I E.M.P.O.W.E.R.

A HEAL KIT INITIATIVE FOR PTSD

27th March 2022

ROE GABRIEL

To my new friend Pamela,
I look forward to many more discussions on life philosophies. I feel we're on the same page with a lot of stuff. I'm interested to get to know you better... and to help you become a kick ass Microsoft user

◆ FriesenPress

Suite 300 - 990 Fort St
Victoria, BC, V8V 3K2
Canada

www.friesenpress.com

Copyright © 2017 by Roe Gabriel
First Edition — 2017

I have recreated events, locales and conversations as I remember them. In order to maintain some anonymity I have changed the names of individuals and places, and may have changed some identifying characteristics, however the content is true to the best of my memory of the events.

All rights reserved.

No part of this publication may be reproduced in any form, or by any means, electronic or mechanical, including photocopying, recording, or any information browsing, storage, or retrieval system, without permission in writing from FriesenPress.

ISBN
978-1-5255-0415-0 (Hardcover)
978-1-5255-0416-7 (Paperback)
978-1-5255-0417-4 (eBook)

1. SELF-HELP, ABUSE

Distributed to the trade by The Ingram Book Company

CONTENTS

Author's Note 7

Foreword 9
   The E.M.P.O.W.E.R. Heal Kit 12

I E.M.P.O.W.E.R. Heal Kit Initiative 1 - Expansion 15
   Expansion in Practice 18
   Victim Vs Empowered Thinking – Tiewin 23

Childhood - Family 28

I E.M.P.O.W.E.R. Heal Kit Initiative 2 - Mindfulness ... 36
   **Important Note: Observation Only 38
   Mindfulness in Practice 38
      Opening the Flood-Gates 38
   Enlightening Shadows 41
      Ingeniously Hidden Judgement 42
   Powerfully Emotional - Accepting Your Reality 46
      Living a Lie for Forty Years 47

Teenagehood - Depression 51

I E.M.P.O.W.E.R. Heal Kit Initiative 3 - Power 55
   Take Right Action 55
      What Does an Empowered Person Look Like? 56
      Spiritual Banking – Internal Power 57
      The Impact of Not Taking Right Action 59
      Take Right Action When Emotion Overwhelms 64
   Taking Responsibility 71

    The House Albatross *72*
    Standing Up - The Fire *75*

Young Adulthood - Missteps **80**
    The Worst Day of My Life 83

I E.M.P.O.W.E.R. Heal Kit Initiative 4 - Others **95**
    True Support 99
        The Phelans *99*
        Supporters Who Don't Even Know Your Name -
        Clara Hughes *100*
    Giving Service to Others 103
        A Moment in Passing *104*

Roaring Twenties And Early Thirties - Self Discovery **108**
    I Belong Here – Finding My People 108
    Theatre Years 113
    Finding Love
    - David - Best Love Ever 114

I E.M.P.O.W.E.R. Heal Kit Initiative 5 - Wisdom **119**
    Insanity – Doing the Same Thing and Expecting Different
    Results 120
    Wisdom in the Pain 120
        What Are You Sensitive To? *121*
        Wise Mistakes *122*
    Noticing Meaning 123
        The Wisdom of Rage *127*
        What Gifts Has My Trauma Brought? *129*

Thirty And Forty-Something - Wheels Falling Off **131**
    Victim's Compensation 135
        The Up-Side *138*
    The Canadian Dream 139

I E.M.P.O.W.E.R. Heal Kit Initiative 6 - Evolution 141
Accessing the Deep Beliefs - Proof of Life 141
- *Abandonment Theory* 145
- *Worthlessness Theory* 146
- *Unlovable Theory* 148
- *Unwise With Money Theory* 148
- *Unhappy Life Theory* 150
- *Shame Theory* 153

Forty-Fied 157
Rheumatology – It's in the Genes 159

I E.M.P.O.W.E.R. Heal Kit Initiative 7 - Resources 162
Integration 163
- *EMDR* 164
- *EFT Tapping* 164
- *Brainwaves* 165
- *Allowing Gratitude* 166
- *Nature* 167
- *Physical Exercise* 168
- *Mental Stimulation* 170
- *Forgiveness* 171

A New Beginning 176
Fifty and Beyond 177

Author's Note

I HAVE RECREATED EVENTS, LOCALES AND CONVERSATIONS AS I remember them. In order to maintain some anonymity I have changed the names of individuals and places, and may have changed some identifying characteristics, however, the content is true to the best of my memory of the events.

FOREWORD

~ True belonging only happens when we present our authentic, imperfect selves to the world, our sense of belonging can never be greater than our level of self-acceptance. ~ **Brene Brown** - *The Gifts of Imperfection.*

WHY AM I HERE? THE ETERNAL SHAKESPEAREAN QUESTION OF "To be or not to be?" At some point we have all succumbed to some version of this question. It is our most vulnerable moment when we question our very existence. When life forces you to ask this question it is really asking, "What are you willing to do to be the best version of yourself?" If we do not allow the openness of truly asking this question without jumping in with a standard answer, then we are missing the true depths of life. What is my dharma? Stop! Don't answer – just listen. What is my purpose in life, on this earth, in this lifetime? Stop! Don't answer – listen. Let it come. What am I willing to do to be the best version of myself?

I stopped to listen.

I was at the brink. This was it for me. *Do I go forward or end everything permanently?* I wasn't asking this dramatically - I was really wondering. We are taught not to wonder about these things, but if I don't ask, then I am living out of obligation, not because I have deliberately chosen this path. I wanted to choose my life. Depending on your beliefs I didn't get the option of being born or not. Well, I may have but I don't recall it. I didn't get the option of choosing my parents, although, once again, I may have, but by the time I realised who they were I didn't get an option to change – there are no return policies. I did not get the choice of whether or not to be abused from a young age. I didn't consciously choose an abusive boyfriend, and given what we know about psychology, I didn't get the choice to break free until it was too late. So at no time in my life did I ever "decide" what I wanted... until 2012. And on that day, I dared to honestly look at how much my life sucked. I had always been trying to convince myself that it didn't, but it was evident that it indeed did.

I paused to listen to my soul.

My main mental health diagnosis is PTSD (post-traumatic stress disorder), but I have been through many: depression, dysthymia, general anxiety disorder, dissociative identity disorder, and probably some undiagnosed ones too. The DSM[1] changes as we gain more insight into the human condition and all it does to the psyche, but at the end of the day, to me it just means life is more challenging. Did what I was feeling have nothing to do with my life? Was it just a label for whichever new mental health definition they decided to give me? I think the label is just another tool to help me figure out a better way forward. All these diagnoses seemed to fit at the time, however, things change, and some of them didn't fit anymore. Yet I was still in pain. Were my feelings just about biochemistry, or was I genuinely trying to get to the bottom of things? I had decided long ago on my journey that it didn't matter what my label of the month was. What mattered in this moment was that I was in pain and I wanted it to stop!

My childhood abuse was followed by abusive boyfriends who raped and beat me, and then this was followed by a gang rape. Eight men that I can recall, maybe ten, maybe more, who raped me and left me to die in the gutter; all arranged by those who supposedly loved me. Obviously, that's not love. But I didn't know that back then. From that time to this I suffered greatly. Was my destiny to feel this much pain? Peace seemed like a much more optimum goal.

Which decision would give me peace? Abusive events had permanently changed my trajectory in life. They had created chaos, rage, and pain and had made my life unbearable at that time.

---

1 Diagnostic and Statistical Manual

On April 1st, 2012, I woke up and I understood that I needed to either choose life or not. If I wanted to go forward, the only way to do it was to heal. As I paused to contemplate this question, I let go of the need to answer it. The second I let go of "needing" the answer, it came. It's counter-intuitive, but sometimes you just need to sit with the question. If you rush to answer before you've given yourself enough time to mull it over, you may come up with a Band-Aid solution that could give you instant relief, but which doesn't last long. It didn't fix everything, but after some contemplation, the answer came resonant and strong: *I want this life.*

On this day I chose my life, for the first time. But I had to wait for that feeling to brew within me.

It was then that I started my journey into true healing. I walked into the wisdom of my shadows. I delved into the nadir and felt my own vulnerability. I realised that my own thinking and feeling was all that stood between me; my authentic self, and me; my damaged and broken self. That didn't mean it felt good and the pain went away, however, I found a way to transform the crippling consequences of severe trauma. I put together my own collection of ways to keep safe, to process, to allow reality to be as it was and be ok with it, and the end result was cathartic.

Just to be clear, I don't recommend being suicidal, as it's destructive in any capacity, however, I am saying, allow yourself to ask the deeper questions of definitively choosing life. Although I was in this pain, I still functioned in a normal life with a job that I went to every weekday. I still had friends and walked my dog. Anything that interferes with regular life needs professional assistance. My book is just another tool toward healing and is in no way to be taken as a substitute for professional help. I am not a psychologist. I didn't study, I just observed my "self" and what my own methods of healing were and am sharing them here.

Some people may not like this story. They may want to put the book down and walk away. I know I wanted to walk away from my life many times, especially the hard times. You may wonder why I would want to share this trauma and healing journey. I'm sharing it because it's my story. It's life, it's real, it's human. So if you want to, just walk away and go enjoy your binge-watching of *Game of Thrones*. That would be much more relaxing…and less violent ;-)

THE E.M.P.O.W.E.R. HEAL KIT

WE HAVE "KITS" FOR ALL KINDS OF THINGS: TOOLKITS, FIRST AID kits, bike wheel puncture kits, camping kits, hockey kits, corporate sales kits, iPhone kits, DNA kits, and emergency preparedness kits. They provide us with the essential components of what we need in our lives at particular moments. It can mean so much and give considerable support; sometimes life saving support. If you don't have one in the pertinent moment, after much cursing and carrying on, "if onlys," and promises to God that if He or She (whichever gender God identifies as) gets us out of this mess we'll never leave home without this kit again, we realize just how much better we could have been prepared for the situation – and these are just sporadic situations. It's amazing we have all these kits for all these emergencies and life situations, yet seldom do we have a life kit for emotional situations, even though it is our emotional experience that greatly informs our daily lives. Sure, we have books and programs and steps and seminars and webinars, but I wanted something more tangible and immediate, rather than just something I visited from time to time; maybe a list that I carried in my wallet of simple steps, or an app I could download to my smart phone in this modern world. If something emotional confronted me, I didn't want to have to wait a week before my next counselling appointment or my next Oprah Soul Session to figure out what was going on and how I could heal it. I was hurting now!

I wanted to come up with a list of initiatives defined by an acronym that I could remember because it was the only thing that stuck. Acronyms work for me so I created one that encapsulated my process for healing. *I E.M.P.O.W.E.R.* The "I" not only represents the self but also stands for Integration, which is the main goal for healing trauma. The rest of the acronym is how to get there.

E.M.P.O.W.E.R.
Expansion   Resources
   Mindfulness   Evolution
     Power   Wisdom
       Others

I can remember at any time how to recall any initiative, just because it's part of an acronym that embodies its purpose. That way, in times of crisis I won't forget it. First aid is full of acronyms. That's because if someone drops dead in front of you, you will probably go into shock and forget everything, except you may remember ABC (airway, breathing, circulation). Just having that in your pocket may one day be useful enough to save a life because your training will come back to you through the acronym trigger. Emotional situations too can cause a type of shock or reactivity that is more primal. So I carry my I EMPOWER healing kit initiatives in my mind's pocket (and my smart phone), ready for any confronting emotional situation and it helps me navigate my life for the better. I practice each step just like running fire drills, so that in the event of an emotional crisis I know what to do without having to think about it. Any sort of crisis management is based on training before the event. Before combat, soldiers run all kinds of drills, while firemen, police, and everyone in highly charged situations prepare well before a "live" event.

When you are overwhelmed with trauma and its emotionally charged consequences, the more training you have in what can be done to relieve the pressure, the better off you'll be.

The beauty of this kit is that it doesn't weigh anything, you don't have to buy it (well, apart from purchasing this book), and no one can see it or tell when you're using it. It has complete anonymity, and you can spend your life adding all the useful tools you find along the way. You don't ever have to leave home without it.

Everyone has steps: 12 steps to sobriety; 7 steps to success; 5 stages of grief; 7 steps to happiness; 10 insights. I have created my own 7 initiatives program for healing from PTSD, trauma, (and related diagnoses), as we humans need to break it down into bite-sized pieces or we get overwhelmed. Our brains are just wired that way. I observed my healing over time and wrote down the main concepts. There are 7 initiatives, each intrinsically entwined with the others. You can't leave any out. Just as in a tool kit, you've got to have certain basic equipment for the job at hand. You don't want to be out hiking the backcountry without a map, a GPS, a flashlight, warm clothes and shelter, food and water, a signalling device and phone, and a knife and fire starter. Well you can if you like - you just won't survive very long if something goes wrong. Each type of kit has the essentials to survive for its purpose. Because my kit is virtual rather than physical, I put the concepts into an acronym just for my own ease of remembering what to do, especially for when I might already be off-balance from intense emotion. It had to be simple.

Having said that, healing is not as easy as it sounds. It's not just about arranging things in order, stuffing them into a virtual bag, calling it a "kit" and off you go. Still, it was vitally important for my survival to put one together. Healing is about plunging into the murky shadows of our emotional secrets and being ok with that. It's about letting go of everything we thought to be true, in order to release ourselves from our own suffering. We are holding on to our beliefs for a reason, usually to protect ourselves, so to let that go is often terrifying. Letting go of these beliefs forces you to question your very being and existence, just as I questioned mine, and at that time you're going to need support.

I.E.M.P.O.W.E.R.
HEAL KIT INITIATIVE 1
- EXPANSION

~ "People suffer because they are caught in their views. As soon as we release those views, we are free and we don't suffer anymore." ~ **Thich Nhat Hanh**

AFTER MY DECISION TO LIVE MY LIFE, RATHER THAN JUST EXIST within it, I realised that the status quo could not remain. My life at the time really did suck. Now, on April 1st in 2017, I have a great job working in wholesale furniture for a global, family-run business that's doing exceptionally well. It's not where I thought I'd be at forty-eight. I wanted to be a police officer or emergency manager and be at the frontline helping people in need, or using my creativity in the entertainment industry somewhere. I am a good singer, and excellent theatre director, but for many reasons those careers never materialized despite several attempts. Even though this job is nowhere near any of the things I thought I loved, it uses all my skills, I have a fantastic boss, and I am a well-respected senior manager in the company. I also love their furniture...and so does my apartment.

Financially, I am recovering well from bankruptcy and am working on regaining my once awesome credit score. I live in the beautiful North Shore Mountains in Vancouver, BC, in my secret oasis that helps me find bliss in any circumstance. I have an assortment of awesome friends. I have best friends from school all these years later. I have work friends who have remained since my early days as a manager. I have spiritual friends and the type of friends you would do anything for, like dive into a freezing, fast-flowing river to save their dog, and they don't mind that you lost your pants around your knees and mooned them on the way out of the water because you just risked your life for their pooch.

All of my friends have one thing in common, (apart from the fact that half of them have seen my butt), they enrich my life in a powerful way. They support me willingly – not to mention the love affair I have with my dog. Yes, I am one of those "dog people." I cuddle up with my furry friend and feel his little heart beating and caress his soft little paws as I watch his eyes close slowly after a hard day's hike. He who doesn't speak says an awful lot. I have learned so much from him.

PHOTO: My dog Sebastien. His favourite things include ball chasing, swimming in the ocean or river but NOT in the bath, and stick chewing.

I love my life so much it makes you want to retch. I have generous amounts of serenity, but it wasn't always that way. In fact, this is the first time in my forty-eight years that it has been so. I am serene, but not because I am healed. I have not, and probably will never overcome all my challenges. What I have learned to do, though, is accept purely where I am, who I am, and where I have come from. It's this that produces the serenity.

Healing is really not about overcoming all your challenges to lead a happy life; it is really about being happy with the life you are leading, with all its complications. This is an important distinction. I used to strive to be better, stronger, and happier. I would read self-help books and truly click with what they were saying, but then I would find disappointment when I couldn't end up like the author where life was blissful. I didn't realise that contentedness can look like pain, it can feel like courage, and it can come in the worst moments of your life.

The 7 initiatives in this process of healing, which facilitated this peace within me certainly didn't happen overnight, or by reading a book or thinking about things. My healing was and still is a process and a way of being that I employ every day just like keeping healthy is a lifestyle choice, not a crash diet.

The first of these initiatives seems obvious, but like all healing concepts, it's simple to understand and difficult to put into practice. *Expand your thinking!* See, doesn't that sound easy? Just like if you want to lose weight, stop eating so many calories and exercise! It seems so simple. Expanding your thinking is also a simple concept, however, it means that you have to let go of what you believe in, to allow for new concepts. You may even need to abandon some beliefs altogether. It is extremely confronting to do this and is very unsettling. Knowing that I was going to feel unsettled helped me be ok with the process. Sometimes it's a positive thing to feel like total crap! It gives you freedom to make changes you wouldn't ordinarily allow, and lets you know that you are in the right place. More often than not we stop going forward with healing because it hurts and we fear we are on the wrong track. This time I let myself believe that the pain was merely a symptom that I was on the **right** path, and I kept going.

Dr. Phil asks about holding on to beliefs that don't support your healing: "How's that working for you?"

Whatever way you choose to heal, whatever you choose to believe, that simple question of "Is it working for you?" can be so powerful. If it were working, then you would be healed already. If not, then something has to radically change in order to move forward. Mostly it is the thinking that needs to change, and then the actions follow naturally. You can't do it in reverse. The mistake most people make is that they go on a diet thinking that it's the food intake they have to change. You can change your food intake all you like, but if you don't change the thinking behind why you craved unhealthy foods in the first place, the change won't stick.

EXPANSION IN PRACTICE

JUST A FEW SHORT YEARS AGO, AFTER HAVING MOVED TO Vancouver, BC, my marriage was a disaster; I was about to lose my house back in Quebec, which I loved so much; I was in a really bad work environment with bullies, who only cared about money; I lived in the drug capital of the universe in Surrey, BC, where RCMP would show up in my apartment building every second day, and I wondered when I was going to be mugged, raped, or caught in the wrong place at the wrong time and killed. I kept failing in friendships because I was so intense, and emotionally I was at rock bottom. Life seemed very bleak. In the depths of my despair I was confronted with a choice to live or to die. I didn't particularly want to die, but living had become so painful I didn't know what else to do. I had tried all kinds of healing methods, counselling, and a variety of natural and medical therapies, and although I'd made great leaps and bounds with breakthroughs and amazing revelations, I always bounced back to depression and anxiety that would not relent. I mean sure, that could have just been related to some mental health diagnosis like depression, or PTSD but even if it was, being victim to that was totally giving away my power. Even though I had suffered major trauma that anyone would feel horrible about, I still believed that if I empowered myself using this healing initiative it would positively influence the outcome of how I felt. Expand your thinking! But what does that look like?

I had left a message for my counsellor that I was in trouble. Some time later, the phone rang. When I answered Will said, "Hey," in his deep, masculine voice. He's six feet four inches with a deep, resonating voice that can sound sincerely sweet at times. His "hey" had compassion and understanding; exactly what I needed in that moment. I cried and it took a little while for me to speak. I had just showered so I was wet and cold and my usually cozy track pants and hoodie gave me no comfort. I stared out the bedroom window at the spectacular mountains that ordinarily soothed me. They were not having the desired effect. Instead they contributed to the overwhelming feeling that I was tired beyond fatigue.

"I've had enough Will."

Will didn't try to "therapise" me. He didn't even try to tell me not to go through with killing myself. I couldn't bring myself to tell him what was laid out in front of me, but he knew how serious I was. In fact, this was the closest I'd come to death since my most devastating trauma twenty-three years earlier; a gang rape. I didn't even feel the need to write a suicide note. Who was I going to write it to? I felt abandoned by the world, abandoned by God and my family, and most of all I was tired of trying to heal. I was forty-three and half years old – you'd think I would have healed by now. I hadn't had any major traumatic experiences for over fifteen years. Why was the depression still lingering?

Will asked me the predictable question of what was going on. What had happened in the two days since I'd seen him in my last session, where I'd seemed fine and feeling good?

The truth is, nothing had happened; no drama, no traumatic experience to speak of – it was just that I'd had enough. "I'm tired of trying to heal, I'm tired of having to deal with my PTSD every day, I'm tired of pushing shit uphill only to have it fall back on me and I have to start over and I'm done!"

Will listened intently.

"I still have to fight my way through the day just to settle my anxiety from whatever the trigger of the day seems to be. There's always something: I can't close my eyes in the shower, I can't catch the SkyTrain without scanning it for potential threats, I can't sit with my back to the door of a café or restaurant, I can't have someone surprise me – can't can't can't! Every day it's something. I even have to filter the TV shows I watch, and it's not like I can follow a set of rules to curb my anxiety. What triggered me yesterday may not have the same effect today. Some days I can watch true-crime murder stories and others the toilet paper ad with the puppy will trigger me into a flood of tears. The roller coaster never ends."

I relaxed a little and lay down on the bed. Will took over for me while I rested, listening to his words in the hope that I would have some epiphany and my whole life would change for the better.

He tried to get to the bottom of why I felt like this. "What's different Roe? What thoughts have surfaced that led to this crisis?"

"Maybe I was never meant to survive such horrific things." I explained that I wasn't feeling this in a despondent way, I was actually questioning. "Maybe I was never meant to get up after being knocked down so many times."

I didn't even want to analyse it. Usually I was all over it, but I just didn't want to engage my brain as I had always done. I usually jumped into action to rescue myself; some healthy actions, some not: *Right, what can I do to feel better? I can go for a walk, I can deal with my anger, I can forgive others, change jobs, change cities, change my environment. . .* the list of things I typically did was long, but I didn't want to do anything like that. I had moved over forty times since I was eighteen. Obviously, this strategy wasn't working for me. This time I just wanted to stop and feel what I was honestly feeling for the first time in a long while.

Will said, "You know what Roe? In the deepest part of my soul, even knowing what I know about you, knowing how much you've suffered; it is my deepest belief that it's just not your time yet. Aside from the fact that it would be a tragedy for you to have come so far and end it like this, years later; I feel like it's just not your time. By all reasoning, you should have died during some of your experiences – but you didn't. Why do you think that is? What would be the point of suffering through all that plus the years of pain since, to end it now? That moment all those years ago that keeps resonating with you, bringing you down, is proof of your strength."

Will's words echoed through my being on every level. When it resonates like that I know it's true.

"What is it that is upsetting you the most?" he said. "Why did you suddenly feel so bad?"

"It's not that sudden. It's like the term 'overnight success'. It usually has many years of hard work before it. I just woke up today and realised that although I get up and go to work every day, breathe in and out all day, the emotion from the gang rape is still there. Hell, the emotions from my father's abuse are still there - every day. Nothing has actually changed, irrespective of the counselling and healing actions I've taken. I just woke up today, years after these events, and realised I hadn't in fact healed. My approach isn't working for me so why am I still doing it?"

Facing this thought took my breath away. I let out a whimper. Hope was gone.

Will said, "I understand why you feel so down about that. I'm not going to tell you what to do or not do - that's your choice, but I will tell you there must be a reason that you survived. My belief is that there must be more to your life than what you can see right now. Maybe it's your beliefs and not your life that aren't supporting your healing."

This is exactly what I needed in that moment. No one telling me to put my feelings away or getting scared that I was going to do something. He didn't label me and dismiss what I was feeling; he just let me feel and stayed with me on the phone while I did it. This was a turning point. Finally, I could categorically make a choice about my life. I didn't have to continue the facade laced with obligation. I didn't have to pretend that I was ok. I wasn't ok and once I acknowledged that, I could start the healing process. Who I was before trauma no longer existed, however, my thinking hadn't yet accepted that until that point even though it was now many years later. If I continue with my dieter's analogy, I was a thin person trapped in big-person thinking as I hadn't accepted my new reality. I had made all the motions, but because I hadn't decided for myself what I wanted, it wasn't grounded. My life had been forever altered by trauma, and it was about time I accepted this fact.

This was my new history and to heal I had to realise my "self" in a new landscape around the changed circumstances. I had to expand who I was before. Most of us retreat and become smaller when trauma occurs. We do fewer things, we enjoy life less, we want to switch off feelings. I had survived severe traumas. If I could get through those, anything else life threw at me could be a piece of cake. These experiences were my fortitude rather than my weakness, but first I had to integrate them. I felt like I was sitting in the consequential pain of my trauma, yet my actual trauma and its experience was sitting in another room somewhere, so I couldn't confront it. Integrating the two was no easy feat, and I hadn't even started for more than twenty to thirty years after the events.

Maybe it wasn't a mistake after all to have survived. Maybe it was exactly part of the plan. Maybe this WAS my life; working out how to overcome my biggest challenges, and if I shared them with others who were struggling, perhaps some good could come of the trauma.

This expanded thinking took me way outside the box. At that moment, I saw it clearly. What if I viewed everything in my life as supportive of my healing rather than as supportive of my being victimised? What if I chose to believe that every event in my life, big or small, was exactly what I needed for my soul's growth?

Deepak Chopra says that our natural essence is always seeking healing even when we're not conscious of it. He says, "The natural force of evolution is a healing force that seeks to rebalance whatever has gone out of balance. This is like biological homeostasis, or even the natural way that our skin heals when we cut it. When we are emotionally hurt, our inner intelligence works to heal it through wisdom and spiritual maturity even if our intelligence and insight isn't always consciously involved."

The clarity hit me. I hadn't been depressed all this time because of some flaw in me. It was the exact opposite. Perhaps since teenage-hood I'd been trying to balance that which had been misaligned by negative experiences growing up. Instead of a weakness it was a strength, only I hadn't delved further to see what it was about, as I was too busy trying to manage the symptom. All the time the pain was telling me something was wrong, only I was ignoring it. Instead of dealing with the cause, I was just dealing with the consequential depression of what was happening. These overwhelming emotions and disconnectedness had been trying to figure themselves out while I lived, and finally, years later they had found the light – a voice, my voice; shaky, strained, yet definitive. The emotions poked through the skin as an overwhelming sense of hopelessness. It was the same feeling of hopelessness I had been avoiding my whole life, which I had assumed was grabbing hold to drown me. But all this time it had been offering me a resting place; trying to save me.

VICTIM VS EMPOWERED THINKING – TIEWIN

IN 2012 I SAW EVENTS IN MY LIFE, BIG OR SMALL, AS INTRUsions; a burden, an unbalanced lack of fairness where every day, I resented having to challenge myself in this way when no one else did, thus keeping me feeling and acting like a victim and in actuality making me more susceptible to being victimised. I had been trying to control the events in my life and was feeling more depressed because I couldn't. I would see even little things that happened negatively. If people didn't let me off the SkyTrain before jumping on, I would feel that I was invisible, and that people were rude and inconsiderate. This would make me feel angry and I would carry that anger to my next life event, big or small. I couldn't see that my mood and the victim's way I carried myself made me less visible to others and encouraged those more dominant to dominate me.

I had previously claimed my victim status, pointing out to various onlookers how much my dreadful life experiences had consumed my present, and it was true to a certain degree. I've had truly appalling life experiences that I'd had no control over, which had caused untold damage that affected my every day. If this was how I viewed my life, why would I want to keep living? I would be crazy to want to stay in it, but that's when that feeling of surrender surfaced. When you totally surrender to something, you allow to it be rather than resist it, and in the midst of that surrender I realised - *This is a good thing*. This dark, horrible feeling; this overwhelming texture of emotion is real. It is my heart directly speaking to me.

It made me pause and think.

I am not a victim. I am now a grownup. I'm forty-something years old and it has been at least fifteen years since my last major trauma. I was no more defined as a victim than I was defined as a pre-schooler. Yes, I had been a victim of serious crimes. That was something that had happened to me, which had changed my life forever. But I could just as easily say that I was a pre-schooler. I had gone to pre-school and it also had changed my life forever. I had an awesome teacher and I made a pillowcase with a gate on it that I carried all my pre-school stuff in. It was just as valid as saying I was a victim and behaving like one. The trauma that had occurred was not a way of life. It was just something that had happened. It was part of my history – not my definition.

What is also not true is not having control of my life at this moment: yes, every day has idiosyncrasies created by some past life event where I have to challenge myself to overcome something and I don't have control over those things coming up, but what I DO have control over is how I react to those "intrusions." It was my victim thinking that I needed to give up – not my life. I needed to let go of the thought that the shroud covering my life was the depression - it wasn't. The depression was my protective mechanism trying to figure out my negative life experiences. It was my step back to view the situation from an unconscious level and figure it out from there, because if I tried to do it consciously, the feelings would overwhelm me and my mind would judge me and it would get nowhere. Being able to go into depression and beyond it to heal was good. I just hadn't realised that before and because of that, I'd never done what I needed to do within the depression, so I never healed.

Every time I feel that twinge of victim thinking, I can just say to myself (and be willing to believe it) that whatever is happening is exactly what I need in this moment for me to develop to be the best soul that I can be. If I acknowledge that anything that happens is there to support me, then I can feel totally differently about those things that occur.

It was empowering as I realised that you cannot heal from the victim's position. Even though it was true I had been a victim of horrible crimes, a victim is not a way of being; it is merely a label for something that has happened. Unfortunately, I had let it define me as a way of being. So when I changed and expanded that thinking, it gave me back control and I empowered myself with a new mantra: the (easy to remember) acronym TIEWIN! This Is Exactly What I Need. This expanded thinking, of believing that everything that happens is trying to support my healing and trying to balance itself is the first tool in my healing kit, and TIEWIN is one way to achieve it.

In the example of the SkyTrain – this gave me an opportunity to project my power – to see if I could make people see me and wait for me get to get off before rushing the train, just by the way I held myself. Let's face it, I needed the practice of presenting an empowered soul. Here was a great opportunity to test it out. Feel brave, stand in my power, and watch to see if people stand aside. I tested this – some days were good and it worked, some days it didn't. But even if it didn't, I was able to view it more positively and think, *It's ok, I get another chance to step into my empowered self tomorrow when I catch the SkyTrain.* When you are healing, every failure just gives you another chance to do it again better next time. And every success strengthens the synapse path in your brain to ensure that if you have been able to achieve it once, you can do it again. The more you practice it, the better you become at it. *This is exactly what I need.* Not – *This proves I am invisible and people are rude and inconsiderate.* What a different feeling I have when I practice this technique. It changes every event in my day to a positive. Yes, it's tiring, but more tiring is feeling like a victim all day, proving over and over again why I am one. Once I tried a technique and it worked, I was then able to adapt that into other parts of my life and it empowered me; it gave me more energy.

This is not positive thinking. I don't believe in the whole fake-it-'til-you-make-it philosophy. I think you need to make a choice to let go of old beliefs and know that what you are currently thinking is not only not working for you – it's downright wrong. If you cannot make the choice to give up your current beliefs, then no amount of faking it is ever going to get you to make it. If you change your food habits without addressing the underlying thinking behind it – then whatever your trigger was for overeating at some point will return, and you will just bounce back to your fat clothes. This is an active choice. I chose to believe that whatever happened was exactly what I needed. Then I sought to prove that theory, and I could always find ways to support it. Just as when I'd chosen to believe my life was crap and I was a victim, I could find ways to support that too and ignore everything else.

So that's the choice. When I wanted to heal I had to ask myself, *Do I want to go with the choice that supports my goal of healing? Or do I support that which continues to victimise me?* Then my revelations started to become transformative rather than just bouncing me back to depression and anxiety. That is true expansion.

Expansion of thinking is the workout phase. It's the aching muscles, too tired to cook dinner phase, and can't brush your teeth because your triceps hurt too much to lift your arm up phase; but when you get fit and healthy - boy does it feel good. It feels good in my relationships, in my work and career, in my self-worth, and in my peacefulness. I don't even want to run from pain anymore - I am excited to see why it's there. What does this mean? What new experiences does the universe have for me with this event? I am, in reality, not a victim; I am empowered beyond my own imagination, and the universe is here supporting my every step, if I can just accept that all of these incidents, big and small, are here JUST for me to realise who I am. If my real goal is to heal, I have no choice but to accept this new belief of TIEWIN. I needed to just be open to the concept, and then allow it to infiltrate my decisions. Over time this expanded thinking influenced me more and more, just by my pausing to ask myself if I was going to approach whatever befell me as victim or an empowered person. Do I EMPOWER? Or not?

CHILDHOOD - FAMILY

I WAS DUE ON MY MOTHER'S BIRTHDAY; I EVEN SENT HER TO hospital in labour pains on the day, but I stopped and thought better of it. Why would I leave such a cozy, warm place in my mom's belly where I got fed whenever I wanted and could sleep all day and had no responsibility? Why would I want to leave perfect bliss where my slate was completely clean, no harm had come to me, no environmental factors had impacted me, and my soul was still pure? So I decided to come a week later after I'd slept on it for a while.

A good Catholic girl, I was born in Sydney, New South Wales, Australia, in 1968 into a regular family with Mom, Dad, an older brother and sister, and a dog and a cat. We had an almost-white picket fence and all the regular kid things; nice neighbours on one side called the Kavanaughs; a grumpy old man next door on the other side, Mr. Avery; friends across the street that we played with until it was too dark to play anymore; and then there was the weird guy up the back, who eventually committed suicide - not that I knew what that meant at the time. It was more a story to bring out at ghost-story time with other kids.

Being a tomboy, I never met a tree I didn't like to climb. I liked to play (rugby league) football against all societal "girls don't do that" rules. Boys would laugh at me when I said I wanted to play. Then they stopped laughing when I crash-tackled them, stole the ball, and scored a try. No activity would beat me. I could climb any tree, ride any hill, swim any ocean and catch any football. I was physically invincible in that regard. In fact, I was always trying to outdo my brother and compete with him. When he got married many years later and I was hanging out playing cricket with him and his friends the night before, he told everyone "stand right back."

They all laughed and moved in with the *girl* hitting the ball. It was only a tennis ball and I smacked the crap out of it right into the chest of one of my brother's friends (by accident of course!)

My brother just laughed and said, "I told you so." He then shared with me that he had always tried to outdo me as a kid, because I was his little sister and he felt he could never compete with me. I'd always thought it was me who couldn't beat him. It's amazing the perceptions you have. I always strived for more and never felt like it was enough. There we were, both of us striving for something we had both already achieved; being enough in the eyes of the other.

I was a curious kid. At age four or five I remember crying because I had fallen asleep in the car right at the moment when we drove out of the rain. I wanted to see what was at the end of the rain. It's not like the rain had stopped, we literally drove out of a weather front and I wanted to see what it looked like. When I woke up we were too far away for me to see the edge. I always wanted to know why and how things worked. Most kids ask the question "Why?" hundreds of times a day. As curious as I was, I kept to myself. I didn't ask why, I just wondered and tried to figure it out for myself. Even in the car when I was crying, when my mom asked why I was crying, I didn't tell her I wanted to see the rain. I just said, "No reason." Apparently, although I don't remember it, my first word was actually a phrase: "Mom did you see that big red ball?" I didn't start with "ball," or "Mom." They probably thought I couldn't talk, but all the time I was just contemplating my own thoughts, and when I thought it was important enough, I decided to share it. Silence was a theme in my life that would repeat persistently.

PHOTO: Mini-me. Aged around five. There's the clothes-line my brother and sister hung me up on and left me on. And that willow tree had taken over the yard when I went back to view the house many years later. The "rapids" used to come out of the garden on the left and stream down the side of the house. Behind the back fence was a little green space where I would play golf with the weird guy at the back.

My Mom had a full-time job and three kids and was finishing her commerce degree. Very smart at school, she topped not just her class, or even her school, but the whole state of New South Wales. Wanting to be a doctor, she ended up as a nurse, as that's what women did at the time, (according to her mother). Doctors who didn't know what they were doing were saved by the fact that she did know. Some doctors would have killed patients by giving the wrong medications in the wrong dosage had it not been for my mom, and for her efforts she was treated like a second-class citizen and was scolded for daring to speak up against a "doctor." That's when she gave up nursing.

After many other professions, Mom got a job in publishing. Working as the only female senior manager at a publishing house, she fought for equality and lost, but she did fight. She got her rightfully earned promotion as marketing manager, however, her career was littered with sexual harassment and sexism. She managed to get a company car like all the other managers, but only after several years of begging. Even the managers below her had company cars. Her win was short-lived, though, as she had to park her car way down the street and walk in so that the men didn't see that she had one. I love my mom and to this day continue to have an excellent relationship with her. It got a bit messy there in the middle, but we are like teenage schoolgirls now when we see each other; squealing with glee and being silly and fun and loving.

I loved my dad too at the time. He was in the navy, and played piano and sang very well. He was fit and athletic and over six feet tall. He towered over my little three-foot body. He took me kayaking and let me sit in the front, and I put my hand over the side to feel the water as it rushed past. I remember how smooth it felt and how warm I felt being with my dad at that time. I was definitely a Daddy's girl. We played tennis, rode bikes, and went for walks for miles to find lighthouses. I was always trying to please my father. My brother and sister weren't that fussed on that, but if Dad asked me to do anything I would do it. I would listen to his music and tell him how wonderful he was. We played on the swings and on the spinning wheel in the playground and would spin so much I would throw up. I never asked him to stop.

My sister Frances, my brother Mark, and I were very creative. We would come up with cheesy take-offs of laundry detergent commercials and other popular culture. We basically performed our own *Saturday Night Live* every week and from my memory of it, we were pretty damn funny. We all had the same sense of humour that Mom shares too. I have fond memories of my brother and me playing in "the rapids." When it rained, a river would form down the side of our backyard and my brother and I would put our wet weather gear on, which consisted of garbage bags taped up so we didn't get wet, and we weathered the storm to watch our home-made paper boats rush down the rapids. It was fun but challenging living with a brother with ADHD. Mark introduced me to the world in a wondrous way; everything was magical and life was at full speed. The downside was I often got hurt. The regular sibling teasing and playing up was also at full speed.

My brother visited me recently; he's now in his fifties and I still can't keep up.

He was saying: "Now that you've finished work, let's go hiking, and then go to dinner, and then. . ." I was happy to see him but I needed a vacation from his stay. The only sign of him slowing down was when he asked, "Can we go hiking without the hills?"

I laughed and said, "I live in the mountains – there's nothing but hills."

There were signs of our upbringing. He couldn't get to sleep without alcohol, and I could see he was under pressure from how he was bringing up his children. He didn't want to give them the same upbringing that we'd had. The scars remain.

Frances was different; she was grown up when I met her. She's five years older than me, and has always been seven going on twenty-one. She was a wild child of a different kind. Sex at thirteen, maybe earlier, unable to process the abuse from Dad, she was quite aggressive and rebellious and became more so as time wore on. She, as an adult, sees the world differently, but not in a fun way like my brother. She has a compassionate side that has helped me in my worst moments, and then at other times she's cold and aggressive and demanding. I can't spend a lot of time with her – not knowing what to expect next clashes with my anxiety.

As a child, I slept in the same room as Frances. I was on the top bunk and she was underneath. Often, in the middle of the night she would need to go to the toilet and she was too scared to go on her own down the darkened hallway, so I would take her, even though I was five and she was ten. I had no fear and I wondered why she did.

As a kid, I was happy; living in the moment, excelling at sports, I was also very clever. I did well at school, played piano at a young age, and liked to sing just like Dad, but there was a dark side in my life. Under my happy, existential existence lay a cancerous turbulence that would colour the rest of my life a darker shade. My father was bi-polar, called manic depression at the time, but I was a kid - I didn't know what that was. In fact, I don't think many people knew what that was at the time. My life was my life; I knew no different. When I got beaten, I assumed like any child that it was my fault and that I needed to try harder the next time. When my father behaved strangely, I trusted that it was what all parents did and it was for my own good. I loved him unconditionally.

We went to the beach a lot, and Dad would "teach" us how to swim. He would hold us under the chin while we were lying on our backs in the water and when a wave came he would give us no notice and dunk us under until the wave passed. He swam us out to beyond the breakers, and then left us there to swim back to shore at five years old. I remember almost drowning on more than one occasion. He "taught" me how to swim very well. I spent forty-something years living beside the ocean and rarely went in it. I tried to be a good girl, but Dad's temper was predictable by the fact that it was unpredictable. It could come seconds after you were laughing with him. He often bashed my brother and sister's heads together when they had done something that he had discerned as wrong, and I still remember the cracking sound. It wasn't a matter of "if" you were going to be hit, only a matter of "when" and how badly. Frances had a game she would play where she would deliberately cause Dad to lose his temper, and she would see how far she could push him until he hit her. I guess it was her way of having some control over the "when."

Dad would say crazy stuff like, "I want my dinner on the table by the time I count three," when it hadn't been prepared yet. He hit my mother in the face across the dinner table for some perceived transgression. When I confronted him about that years later he said, "I never hit your mother across the dinner table. . . it was always in the bedroom," like it made a difference which room he hit her in. Sanity was not a regular occurrence at home, however, Dad had enough of it to convince everyone else how charming he was, and if we misspoke about him people would not befriend us anymore and would console our "poor father" for having such a terrible, unsupportive family. He was a pillar of the church community and gave them cash donations, but then Mom had to scrounge money just to buy us enough to eat. Despite his clinical diagnosis, I'm certain of his manipulation, as he was always being heralded at church for being so "giving," presenting to them the perfect role model while hiding his true aggression. This made my Mom's job of leaving him harder. She got no support from their family and friends or the church. Oddly enough I am no longer affiliated with any religion or church.

One day, Mom had a talk with us and asked us if we wanted to leave Dad. We all said yes without hesitation. She let us know that it had to be our secret, for fear of retaliation. We had to be *silent*. She must have been terrified. She even said we might have to change our names and go somewhere new where he could never find us.

I came home from school and my brother ran to me and said, "Dad is crying." I didn't believe him as he was always, shall we say, "creative" when he relayed information. I certainly didn't believe that Dad was crying. Then my brother relayed that our mom had taken the precaution of taking Dad (as well as his rifle) to the police station where she then told him that we were leaving. She had pre-arranged this with the police. She didn't want to take the risk of telling Dad at the house where he could go into a rage and kill us all for wanting to leave.

When my brother told me the whole story, I didn't feel anything except shock that Dad was crying; I had never seen him cry. I didn't even know he could. I would like to say that I was shocked about hearing how Mom had taken Dad and his rifle to the police station to tell him, but I wasn't. Police and Dad's rifle were part of my regular life as a child.

Even though I knew this at the time, I never questioned the actions of my father. I didn't even know that other families weren't like this. I also didn't know that some other families were. It wasn't until we moved out that I realised that life was different for us. My understanding was that I loved my dad unconditionally. It made it harder for me when his temper came out. I blamed myself and took it really hard, and when we left I felt really torn. He was my first love, and really, I never got over it. I didn't know that this was not what love really was. I spent the next forty years recovering from this relationship and the consequences of it.

We moved into an apartment and changed schools, but we didn't change our names (for my sister and I, that came later, and my brother and I changed countries.) We still saw Dad on some weekends by law, as of course Dad's support in the courthouse outweighed Mom's, so she lost the battle to save us from further infliction of pain and suffering. He never paid alimony because he claimed he was poor due to my mother's leaving. He wrote on Christmas cards, "Sorry kids, no money for gifts this year, why don't you come and visit me on my new yacht!" If he were sane he may have seen the ridiculousness in that. Even as an eight-year-old, I could see the incongruence. My brother and sister were supposed to come with me on weekends, but they hardly ever did. First my sister stopped coming, and then my brother. I didn't like going by myself. The older I got, the less I wanted to see him. Eventually I stopped going altogether, but it was a few years later. By the time I was fifteen, I never wanted to see him again. The fantasy of my "wonderful dad" had been shattered. I missed it, or at least the illusion of it.

The development of how I would interact with the world was done. My formative years were over, and I had been good student of my life and where I fit in. It would take me another thirty years to unravel these foundations that were etched into the fabric of my being. Having said that, all the tools I needed to achieve healing were within me the whole time. What I came into the world with was the most important. It got clouded by the environment, but in my quiet moments it was this spirit of who I genuinely am that I was connecting with to figure it all out. Often we go searching for that elusive thing "out there," that will help our healing. We are looking for that inner peace, when all the time it is and always will be within us. When trauma impacts us, it's often hard to get back to that place of peace that we entered the world with – but it's there.

I E.M.P.O.W.E.R.
HEAL KIT INITIATIVE 2
- MINDFULNESS

~ "Vulnerability sounds like truth and feels like courage. Truth and courage aren't always comfortable, but they're never weakness." ~ **Brené Brown**, *Daring Greatly: How the Courage to Be Vulnerable Transforms the Way We Live, Love, Parent, and Lead*

DISSOCIATION IS YOUR FRIEND WHEN YOU ARE IN A TRAUMATIC experience. It is an excellent tool to be able to put aside feelings that are too overwhelming to deal with at the time and save them for a later date. The problem is, no one wants to open that door to extreme feelings, pain, and vulnerability later, so those healing from trauma tend to avoid it. We lock it away in another room in our minds in the hope that no one sees our true vulnerability. The problem is that it starts leaking into your daily life. It permeates your soul and affects every decision, whether it be to avoid certain things or to dull the pain somehow. MINDFULNESS is the opposite. It is experiencing everything in the present moment, embracing your vulnerability in order to heal whatever comes up, and getting in touch with who you really are. There are times when dissociation is helpful, but mindfulness is imperative to be able to heal from trauma. Healing is about integrating with your experiences. Dissociation disconnects you to keep you safe, but to heal, you have to knock down the walls of that locked room and integrate it with your wholeness.

Mindfulness pulls together all of who you are; from your most vulnerable thoughts and feelings, to your most authentic truth. Many conventional treatments for emotional and mental ailments, many spiritual practices, and most positive healing approaches, include mindfulness. In my experience you cannot heal without it. It is once again a simple concept, yet difficult to execute. In its simplest form, for me it is: Listen to your heart and soul and they will guide you through anything in life; don't listen and you will suffer repeatedly.

Your past feelings will continue to display in your present until you have integrated them. Once you commit to healing and open your mind to expand it, mindfulness will be a necessity to deal with what follows, and the gifts that emanate from it are very healing. It's good practice to "check in" with how you're feeling at least once a day, if not more, otherwise our clever minds can find ways to ignore and deny how we really feel.

Once I opened to a new way of thinking, the things that were keeping me stuck in the old ways surfaced and caused great unrest. Expansion is a great button pusher. It didn't feel good. So what now? In the philosophy of TIEWIN, that's great! That meant that now, having felt the disturbance, I was on the right track, but I needed a way to deal with whatever came up. The deeper the trauma or experience that kept me stuck, the more painful it was when it came back up. My thinking was built around my protection from painful memories and feelings that at the time were necessary; but what once protected me, was now holding me in the status quo of unhealed limbo. When you're in protection mode, you have no choice but to distract yourself from your real feelings. It's a great tool, used at a moment of trauma when the feelings are too overwhelming to deal with, but protection is only ever meant to be temporary. Some people set up camp there for life, and their denial causes them huge turbulence in every facet of their lives, however, that is still more appealing to them than delving into the depths of intense emotion.

**IMPORTANT NOTE: OBSERVATION ONLY*

One rule is that mindfulness is observation only. You don't get to "do" anything, (that's heal kit initiative number 3.) It's like being an intern; you are there to absorb knowledge: Look but don't touch; watch but don't speak; listen intently and process; but don't act. It is a path to feeling what comes up, and giving it a voice, nothing more, or less, and when you quieten your need to "do" something, it allows the real feelings to arise. If you do something during the mindfulness, you may not hear the whole message. You may act without knowing the full story, and you may act in a way that you regret later. Feelings won't kill you, but acting on them might. Wait for the water to even out on either side of the flood-gates. Then you can act.

MINDFULNESS IN PRACTICE

OPENING THE FLOOD-GATES

I met my wife in 2009 while working in Ottawa. After a while we had decided that Ottawa was a sleepy, government town, and although it was pretty, it was also dull. I missed the ocean. Having grown up always near one, it was a difficult adjustment for me to be landlocked. My wife wanted to leave her ex-Jehovah's Witness life behind and start fresh somewhere else, as obviously, being gay was not congruent with that lifestyle. So we packed up and shifted across country to Vancouver, BC.

I had convinced myself that this relationship was my everything. Finally I was able to express my true sexuality. I was euphoric.

The honeymoon soon wore off. Even though doubts started to creep in, I convinced myself it was all in my head; I was just being too sensitive.

I am under no delusion that I was easy to live with either; still fighting the depression and anxiety while avoiding my vulnerability and not living my truth. Of course the relationship was doomed, it would just be a matter of time. The constant underlying discomfort that I had thought was location-related began to niggle well after our settling down in BC. That little voice inside my head that tells me when something is off, started to get louder. It became so loud that one day I blurted out: "I'm done! I want out!"

Ok they were not the words I'd had in mind, but that's how it came out. I had been in pain physically, emotionally, and spiritually for quite some time. In the lead up to my outburst, six weeks earlier, I'd had a cathartic moment. I spent New Year's Eve 2012 flat on my back, unable to move with a severe back-ache. I was depressed and was getting so bad that it was being reflected in my body as its muscles spasmed out of control. Gripped in pain, I lay on my back staring at the ceiling of the kitchen where I had collapsed, waiting for the painkillers to settle in, and seeing if I needed to get an ambulance or not. I realised that this was my wake-up call. This was exactly what I needed. I had been in denial for so long now I had forgotten what I actually felt. Then my body cleverly forced me to stop all the running around and avoidance tactics. I had no choice but to be mindful while I lay there for days recovering from my back seizure. When I lay in bed that night in terrible agony, with my wife beside me, I waited for the new year to begin, hoping it would be better than the last. I wondered what I could do to make it so. I cried to myself and just listened to what my body was telling me. Something was wrong in my life.

I reflected on everything in my life; my relationships, my body, my job, and my sense of well-being. I assessed everything and I opened to the emotions that were there. I opened the flood-gates to my vulnerability and let it all out so that my heart could tell me the truth. What was really going on with me? This was true mindfulness, although it only became that dramatic because I had ignored all the whispers before that.

From New Year's until around February of 2013, I felt myself slipping further and further away and then there I was; just a shell. My self-esteem had diminished so much from staying in an unhealthy relationship that I felt I almost didn't exist anymore. It took a couple of months from when I was lying on the floor of the kitchen to the point where I blurted out, "I want out!" but I knew in my heart it was time. Without making my commitment to expand my thinking, I probably could have stayed in the marriage; unhappy, but still in it. It was due to the fact that I devoted myself to really healing that I knew I couldn't just maintain the status quo. This time, I had stopped to listen, but there were many other times when I hadn't.

There was nothing dramatic; no huge issues, no continuous arguments – there was just this sense for me that I was never enough and I already felt that way internally. I didn't want it reinforced by my partner. I didn't like who I was any more, and I didn't like how the relationship made me feel. I was mindful of how I felt, and in a relationship if you don't like who you are while you're in it, you can be fairly certain that it's not healthy, whatever the reasons for feeling that way. It's impossible to heal while you're still holding on to a past that is already over. My marriage had been over for quite some time, all I needed to do was acknowledge it. So I stepped into the void.

After I told Angie we were done, I was so distressed. I hurt like crazy and the next couple of weeks before she went back to Quebec to be with her family were excruciating – I missed her so badly even though she was still in the house. I opened my heart and let it bleed. I felt my vulnerability, I drew breath in and out every day, and I went for coffee with supportive friends and just digested my situation and its consequential feelings. Everything in the moment felt fragile, but I just allowed the feelings to come through, welcomed them, and felt them course through my veins. I sat peacefully on my sofa after having told Angie in the terribly inauspicious way that we were done, and I allowed the suffering in to my whole body, mind, and spirit. I could almost feel my own heart beating, and I felt that I had just dissolved some of the barriers around it. It left me completely open, and hence, able to heal. This is the best form of healing; to welcome your emotions no matter how intense, vulnerable, or negative, because then the door will remain open for the positive.

A few days passed on my own after Angie left and suddenly I felt self-esteem that I had never experienced. I felt so empowered and knew I was doing the right thing. The amount of joy and peace was directly proportionate to the amount of pain I had allowed myself to be mindful of. That's how mindfulness works. Those who truly have inner peace are those who are most able to sit with the discomfort and allow it to breathe. This was exactly what I needed.

You don't need something so dramatic to be mindful; you can do anything mindfully. I can eat this piece of chocolate cake mindfully, knowing it will triple in size once it reaches my butt, however, being mindful will decrease my chances of going back for a second or third piece. It is truly opening up all your senses, including your sense of being in the world and seeing how you are truly interacting with it. And if you pay attention to what you feel through all your senses, your soul will clearly speak to you about what's going on. If you don't listen, it will yell at you, and if you choose to ignore it, it will flatten you on your back either metaphorically or literally if you are not paying attention. Being mindful isn't really a choice. You will suffer the consequences if you don't hear your voice. Being mindful is really about the choice to listen to what is being said. The deep, inner voice that mindfulness brings you to, will always be there. Mindfulness is just learning how to switch off the other sounds so you can hear it better. Once you hear the message clearly, you will be able to make clearer choices about what to do next. When you do listen, the gifts of the world are brought to you. The peace you were searching for arises, as does the self-confidence and all those cool things we crave. Love is abundant. Just don't expect it to feel like that immediately, but it will come.

ENLIGHTENING SHADOWS

~ "Unless you learn to face your own shadows, you will continue to see them in others, because the world outside you, is only a reflection of the world inside you." ~ **Anonymous.**

THE THING ABOUT MINDFULNESS IS THAT WHEN YOU START IT AS a practice, you get in touch with who you are and what you are feeling, and you become present with those feelings. When you start to do that, feelings that you never knew existed begin to rumble. Even more confronting than events that happened to me, was confronting my own inner demons. We all have our shadow selves, and more often than not, the things we criticise in others are the very things we recognise in ourselves at a subconscious level, which is why they trigger such an emotionally-charged response. When you start to peel back the layers of distraction, you see yourself more truthfully, and some of it is not pretty. In the essence of TIEWIN, the best thing to do is embrace your shadows without judgement. Don't judge others or yourself.

INGENIOUSLY HIDDEN JUDGEMENT

We are so ingenious that we have even found a way to take a jab at ourselves while hiding it from ourselves. How clever are we that we can judge others and think we are safe from judgement's slings and arrows, when all we are really doing is judging ourselves and feeling it in our hearts. So clever, yet so destructive, and until we face those shadows they will continue to present themselves in our lives. If we pay attention through mindfulness, then we can get a map of how we are feeling at any time and what we still need to work on. Me judging people for little things, or even bigger things, is my way of identifying what I haven't come to terms with yet, within myself.

As Tom Cruise jumped up and down on Oprah's sofa to express his undying love for his now-defunct relationship with Katie Holmes, he was slammed by the media. We pay him millions of dollars to scream, "Show me the money," to be loud and passionate and reckless with emotion, but the second he shows anything real, we turn and judge and condemn. I may not agree with what Mr. Cruise's decisions have been over his children or his choice of religious beliefs or the way he treated his wives, but jumping on a couch is not something to blow up in the media; especially when we demand of him to do just that to produce what he does for a living. Would anyone be sliding across the floor in his or her underwear and socks if Tom Cruise had casually walked across the floor in *Risky Business*? Would anyone have cared about that movie? I think not. Let judgement be for those times when someone is being harmed or negatively affected, not for someone jumping on a couch saying how much he loves someone.

We haven't yet found a balance here of what to judge and when. Judgement is so devastatingly destructive that it can even kill. Teen suicides are often driven by it. People's fear of coming out as gay is created by it, and many more things in life are coloured by our own judgement of ourselves as a whole society and as individuals. Having said all that, lurking in the twilight of judgement is truth. It can be your best ally in mindfulness. You can see the truth in what you personally judge. You can also see what others are feeling just by what they are judging. If we turn it around and look at judgement not as something to fear but as something to acknowledge, it is so revealing. Aha! That's why that happens! Find the balance of healing judgement. Use it as a tool to heal, not to destroy. It's a simple rule.

I.T.: "Just reboot it."

ME: "I already tried that, it's not just my computer, it's everyone's."

I.T.: "Ok. Just reboot the server."

ME - *OMG these people are annoying. Just do your job, you moron! If it was as simple as rebooting something, I would have done it already.* (Ok, I didn't say that but I was thinking it and it was reflected in my tone.)

Haven't we all experienced that I.T. moment when of course we have already tried rebooting it? Four years of university and all you can come up with is reboot it? Really? However, my negative reaction not only affects me, but also indicates my own pain of frustration about people not listening to me and not being truly helpful. When I was growing up and was struggling with abuse and pain, people would tell me, in effect, to just "reboot it, get over it, move on." That pushes a button that isn't just the on/off switch of a computer. It is a feeling that whoever is "helping" is not actually bothering to find out what's really broken and doesn't care enough to really listen to help you solve the issue.

Fat person gorging on a second hamburger.

Me - disgusted and judgemental. It's just a thought, but even a thought has an energy and a voice and a consequence. I am no skinny Minnie. I have a few spare tires around my middle, and when I judge others for how big they are and what they eat, it's my own inability to stick to a healthy diet that disgusts me. I kid myself that I eat healthy…and I do eat healthy, but then I add to it bucketloads of chocolate, and ice-cream and wonder why I am not losing weight.

Team member at work not doing something efficiently and taking three times longer than needed.

Me – feeling controlling and wanting to make them do it my way, even though they still get there in the end. Once again, it's a thought that gets reflected in my tone when I talk to them; passive aggressive comments slip out.

A car trying to get across an intersection and blocking traffic going my way.

Me - angrily yelling at the "stupid idiot" even though he can't hear me and even though I had done the same thing minutes before at the last intersection.

I am judgemental every day at little annoyances like these, and every time I am like this, I hinder my own healing and growth. It doesn't look like rage (yelling at the traffic or being passive aggressive occasionally), but if I do it consistently enough it tips the scale over into being more than disgruntled.

My hardest time has been realising just how much rage I still have after all these years. Rage is a natural by-product of trauma and when I am mindful and see what I am judging, I can see that it's really just misdirected rage. I thought that because I wasn't punching walls and I wasn't yelling and screaming every day, then I didn't have rage; I was fine! But that's just it; most of my day was filled with these little annoyances, which were actually uncontrolled mini-rages directed at "stupid people." My complaining about stupid people in the world is not healthy for anyone. It has no positive meaning, but who am I really judging?

Of course the only stupid person I was referring to was me. Way back in my deep, dark history was the thought: *How dumb am I to be with an abusive boyfriend at the ripe old age of seventeen?* I didn't even get out of the starting gate before my first real boyfriend turned nasty. It's not like he suddenly displayed that behaviour; there were many signs. Had I been mindful at the time I would have done something about it, but at seventeen, I wasn't that emotionally evolved. So anytime I felt that people were being inconsiderate, it struck a discord within me – understandably. Not just a small pang, but a real jolt of anger that seemed innocent enough: a yell at the traffic; a passive-aggressive comment; a judgement. Rage haunted me every day, I had just become proficient at hiding it well enough to be "acceptable" in society; not great, or positive even, but it is widely accepted. Judgement is such a great tool, it can highlight to you exactly where you are with rage or anger and give you a heads-up on what you may need to still work on.

Being mindful at these moments instead of being judgemental helped me identify those things I still had yet to work on. Judgement was and still is my ultimate hurdle and ally to admit my shadows. When you feel judgemental, it is much more empowering to believe that the button being pushed is within you and under your power. If you believe that the "stupid" people of the world are to blame, then it is not under your control, you cannot change or fix it, and you will be forever pushed by the will of others. That is not empowering. Choose to believe what will support your healing. Judgement means your pain is being triggered, so deal with your own pain and the button releases.

Now that's different than having a considered opinion. It is my considered opinion that Charles Manson is not a nice man and that Donald Trump would not make a good president. (I wrote these words long before he actually became president.) These are my opinions developed over time, after I'd assessed the situations. A swift judgement of the jerk who cut me off in traffic is not a considered opinion; it is an instant judgement. Cutting someone down because he or she is successful at something or is a teenager driving a Lexus, while I, in my forties still can't afford one, is a judgement and is not healthy. Even Jesus (apparently) said: "Let he who is without sin cast the first stone." The Bible. John 8:7. (Ok, maybe a little of the Catholic upbringing stuck... but not much.) I do not have the right to judge people in this way - it is really my own shadow. However, judging *myself* for my judgemental behaviour is also not supportive of healing either, so I have to forgive myself for having affected those around me.

Next time you are the one jumping on a sofa to profess your love for someone and you feel the weight of others judging, you should understand that it is merely about them and their journey. Pay attention, you might learn what makes them tick. When you see what they are judging - it tells you what they need to work on as well. Don't take it on board as an insult. Judgement gives you insight to yourself and others. Don't use it as another way to victimise yourself.

POWERFULLY EMOTIONAL - ACCEPTING YOUR REALITY

IT'S HARD TO WELCOME HORRIBLE FEELINGS, ESPECIALLY WHEN you've just been through a terrible trauma. It's going to take some time. You can't get over the death of a child or parent or spouse the next day, just because you have been mindful of how you feel. It's a process. What mindfulness does free you from, is the suffering from not accepting your reality. A lot of our suffering comes from the replaying of the incident over and over, hoping it has a different outcome. I have a friend whose son died, and he replays over and over in his sleep, the moment he went in to check on his son in his room. All the "if onlys" come out. *If I had gone in earlier, if I had done CPR properly*, and the list goes on. This is getting stuck in not accepting your reality. Once you have accepted that he is dead and nothing you can do now can ever change the outcome, you will release yourself from this suffering. You will still need to grieve and forgive, but you can't even begin to heal unless you have accepted your reality…even if it's really painful. The reality here is that he will still be dead tomorrow, and even if you had gone in sooner, or done CPR, it doesn't guarantee that it would have changed the outcome. It's as valid as saying - *What if I'd never had a son?* What ifs are merely a tool to help us process, but you must force yourself to move on at some point. The replay is just another way to avoid feeling the true authenticity of the grief. You can stave it off a little if you hold down the replay button, but then the temporary process becomes destructive rather than constructive. It is a process in order for you to figure out what went wrong. Once you realise what went wrong, you need to forgive yourself and move forward. Not forget, and not move past – just integrate.

Mindfulness of this kind gives an opportunity to empower any lost soul. The best gift you can give yourself is that of mindfulness to accept your reality, even if that reality is that you are extremely sad for your loss and it hurts. If you don't move through the pain, then you have very little hope of healing from it. You can't heal from something if you don't acknowledge its existence.

Meditate, go for a walk in nature, breathe, swim, rest, go on a retreat, whichever way you choose to be mindful, do it. There are thousands of books on it, but whichever ways you choose, it has to resonate for you. My favourite book on it is a *Time* magazine special called Mindfulness. It pulls together all the science and concepts into one and tells how to integrate it with our reality of working and being.

I'm an outdoorsy girl, so nature will always bring me back to calm, but that won't work if you're a bookworm who likes cuddling up on your sofa, reading and contemplating life. The "how" doesn't matter, the "what" does. Don't get caught up in the thinking that because you're on a yoga retreat you are being mindful...it all depends on what you're doing within your mind at the time. Mindfulness is the epitome of present-moment awareness in its fullness, using all of your senses. Your present may not always be pleasant, but the more mindful you are and the less you act on it, the more peace you will bring to yourself.

LIVING A LIE FOR FORTY YEARS

Another aspect of mindfulness is being true to who you are; listening to your intuition and honouring your mind, body, and spirit. Had I done this earlier, I could have saved myself years of heartache. In 2010 after meeting my future wife, I had an enlightening discussion with my mother:

"Hi Mom! I have something to tell you."

"You're pregnant?"

"No!"

"Phew! Then, you're gay?"

"Well, yeah."

SILENCE - My heart was now pounding through my chest awaiting my mother's response. Would she reject me? Would she not want to see me again?

She broke the silence with: "Well duh!"

Shocked, I asked, "How long have you known?"

"Since you were about twelve."

"Why didn't you say something?"

"Would you have listened?"

"Of course not!"

Coming out to my mother was easier than expected. In fact, it wasn't that difficult coming out to anyone. After this dialog with my mom I outed myself on Facebook. Positive comments poured in. I seemed to be the only person who had an issue with it. I think I've been gay all my life but was never willing to admit it to myself. There were plenty of signs. I mean – PLENTY! Each one was vigorously denied and ignored by me. I had had a kind of weird fling, if you can call it that, with a woman when I was young, but I was so screwed up at the time and it was such a dysfunctional relationship, that I think if a chimpanzee had shown me any kind of love and affection he (or she) would have been the love of my life at that moment. I couldn't tell which way was up, let alone if I was gay or straight, and I don't think it mattered at that point either.

So up to 2009 I was only attracted to men, but in 2009 I went through this weird phase of not being attracted to them, although I wasn't attracted to women yet either. *Great!* I thought. I was going to end up celibate in a limbo between gay and straight for the rest of my life. It was really weird. I don't know if I was just in such strong denial that it didn't allow me to feel attracted to women, or if it just hadn't quite developed yet. I mean I'd never had success with male relationships, but it's not that I couldn't orgasm, I could – it just didn't feel good. It was forced and uncomfortable. Even the obvious physical sensation was dulled somehow. I had two speeds: completely devoid of feeling, or too much feeling and I would burst into tears and cry uncontrollably for five minutes or so (both PTSD reactions). Even my wonderful soul-mate David (whom we'll talk about later) could not break this format. He was the closest I came to enjoying a sexual experience with a man, but it was more the emotional connection, not the physical one.

I went into sexual status limbo. I wasn't straight as I certainly wasn't attracted to guys any more, but the thought of cuddling up to a woman repulsed me. *What do I do now?* I even tried to find women attractive. I quite like Ellen DeGeneres as a person (as much as you see on TV), but the thought of kissing her felt yuck. At this point though, I did strongly suspect I was gay. (I don't like the word lesbian. It has so many negative connotations that I can't even bring myself to say it, but that's what I am.)

During Vancouver's Winter Olympics in 2010, I was watching from Angie's place in Ottawa. It was so subtle and gentle. I was trying to avoid being attracted as I was her boss at the time, but soon I was swept away again by the intense feelings of opening up myself to who I really was. We kissed lightly and her lips were so soft it almost didn't seem real. I loved her body; its shape and how it felt and just the emotional interaction in an intimate way was more sensual and beautiful. I really hadn't felt anything like it. I couldn't have even imagined it. In that moment, I absolutely confirmed that I was gay, and I knew I would never be with a man again. I called my mother.

Relationships are hard enough as it is without the added pressure that society doesn't accept you. I can't imagine a force big enough to prevent me from accepting myself for who I am for forty years. I spent all that time trapped in relationships I didn't understand with people I didn't want to be with; all so I could fit in and feel accepted. I mean I was attracted to them, so to me it felt real at the time but deep in my heart it whispered, "This is wrong." And why? Was I accepted? Well, actually no. I was just weird. Yes, I see the irony. I can't even say it was peer pressure or pressure from an unwilling family or friends. Really, everyone I knew was ok with me being gay (as far as I know) except me! I wondered what other things lurked under the surface of my beliefs that were interfering with my life because I wasn't being my authentic self. I was sure there were more. I hoped to discover them all and heal and live my own life by being mindful of when my heart felt that inner twang that something was off. I hoped I could once again ask myself what decision would support my healing. I didn't really want to be gay, but I am. Denying that was only going to support my feeling of disconnection with my life.

PHOTO: Me aged fifteen to sixteen-ish, very focused on my tennis, although I am wearing the t-shirt from sailing club. I wish I had that body now! And yes I thought I was fat at the time. I also think I was the same height I am now.

Teenagehood - Depression

MOM REMARRIED A NICE MAN. WHEN I WAS ABOUT TEN YEARS old, the four of us moved from our tiny, one-bedroom apartment after leaving Dad, into a self-designed, beautiful house in Sydney's upmarket North Shore. It was a bit of a shock to the system, but it was a nice shock.

Gordon was to become my stepfather for the next thirty-five years, although that too came with challenges. He had two daughters of his own; one the age of my brother, the other the age of my sister. I suddenly became the youngest of five, and we were no Brady Bunch. My stepsister's mother had abandoned them. She was around – she just didn't want to live with her kids. I never got the real story behind that, despite having spoken with their mother on many occasions. And us? Well I told you already what we had come from, and because we had moved into their house, we were the underlings. It was a difficult situation on all fronts, however, I am grateful that a man would marry my mother given all the baggage. I didn't think about that at the time of course.

At nine or ten I did what I was told, but at eleven and twelve I started to question that philosophy as my body awakened. Teenagehood is bad enough as it is with raging hormones already putting me off balance, but depression had already grabbed hold by around age fifteen. Not only that, my shadows were silenced. Mom, afraid to lose her new, non-abusive husband, verbally gagged us all and told us to *silence* the past. I would stare for hours into the flame of the gas heater we owned, watching it dance. Confused and suppressed, I had nowhere else to go but into anger and depression. I know it's in a teenager's job description to be confused and down, but I seemed to be a little off the regular scale. No one seemed to notice, though, because I could still be happy on the outside. Anyone who did dig deeper was deflected by my mother.

"She makes up lies." "No, that never happened, we had a great past."

My mother even held onto the fact that my brother had once told her he'd had a "happy" childhood. She would mention it often, especially if I said the opposite. I could tell my mother a story that she had told me in previous years, and she'd suddenly deny that it had ever happened, even though it was she who'd told me about it in the first place. She's a little more grounded now. My stepdad has passed and there's nothing to lose. The honesty brought us closer together.

Despite all those obstacles, I had a balance of positive things. I did have the depression, but I rarely showed it to anyone outside of my house. I had fun with my friends, went sailing, excelled at sports at National Championship level, and got good grades at school. It's not like I didn't enjoy life – I did. My stepdad was rich, so we lived in a beautiful house. I went to a good school, and I had many freedoms that others didn't. My music helped too. I'd almost go into a trance playing the piano for hours, writing songs, and playing my favourites over and over, much to the distraction of everyone else in the house. It was good that I had that, however, it was an escape from an already tumultuous inner self. As a child, I'd had a turbulent environment, but I felt happy. As a teenager I had a relatively good environment but was very unhappy on the inside. The negatives had caught up with me.

Mom did send me to a psychiatrist when I was around age sixteen. He was nice; he didn't push too hard. We talked about superficial things. Eventually I got tired of the game and said, "You know all the things I bring up about my troubles at school, being an outcast, and family problems are really all things I can deal with myself. I'm not really getting anywhere."

The psychiatrist said, "I've noticed a few things: When I mention boys or your dad, your eyes glaze over. That tells me that it's what you really need to talk about."

I paused. This was a resonant moment; one where I could facilitate some of that healing, but I simply wasn't ready. At sixteen, I wasn't equipped to know how to deal with my emotions if they did come up. So

I did my best to protect myself. I told the psychiatrist that I knew what he meant about the glazed-over eyes, and I knew why, but that I just wasn't able to share it with him yet. Then I told him we were done.

For the first time he pushed. He begged me to stay and change my mind and come back to talk about it. I never did.

I don't know if the boy thing was to do with being gay or the abuse I suffered from my father. I do know the "Dad" thing was from my terror from childhood. I suffered terrible nightmares, all to do with his physical and emotional abuse. I had become my sister and was now afraid of the dark. The last thing I was ready to do was tell someone about it. So I went back to being a surly teenager; going to school, having fun, and being weird.

Some relationships with friends were really solid. One of these friends I am still friends with to this day. Some relationships were more like idolisation. I had platonic crushes on older people. Because of my confused boundaries I think it came across as sexual, but it never was. Once again at the time, I saw my idolising as another weirdo factor, when actually if I look at TIEWIN, it was a healthy reaction to an unhealthy situation. My family dynamics were horrible on all fronts, so I tried to create role models for myself. Now, the execution of it was messy, however, the principle was good. I chose creative, talented, older people and would idolise them. I tended not to have celebrity crushes, but ultimately it was the same thing. When I started exploring my sexual feelings I did then get some celebrity crushes. (I still have a crush on Richard Dreyfuss. It's just that now Jodie Foster has been added to my celebrity crush mix.) I believe that it was my way to explore those feelings at a distance to test the waters as it were. No porn movie-type fantasies, no, my sexual crushes were limited to having a close discussion about life with them. I did focus on how it made me feel inside though. I believe I was being blocked from really exploring my sexuality, even in fantasy. The thought of being truly sexual was terrifying for me. No boys were asking me out, and no girls either, although I wouldn't have been into that back then. I think I had a big "DANGER DON'T GO NEAR THERE" sign on my forehead.

Then it happened. When I was seventeen, my best friend from school wanted me to go to a party with her. I was not a party-type girl, but I had promised I would go. She even called me after the party had started and said, "Where are you?" After I tried to get out of it Emma convinced me that I had to go. I was primed for meeting the wrong guy. Still in idolisation mode, I talked to a few people, and then this one guy caught my eye. He seemed really interesting. He was about five years older than me, which at that age is HUGE. He was sophisticated, intelligent, and seemed to really like me. I was an easy catch.

No sex for a long time, however, I was hooked by the amount of attention I was getting. I felt that urge to grow up. I would be leaving school soon, and I wanted some independence. He was charming and telling me all the things I wanted to hear. His name was Peter. In a heartbeat I seemed to be moving out of home to live with him. (A clear sign that I was in no way ready for such a relationship.) I listened to no one, not even myself. And as much as some things felt wrong, my heart was receiving some stroking. Two dysfunctional people coming together, attracted by their mutual, subconscious yearning fill each other's need. It was a disaster in the making. This relationship with Peter punctuated my teenagehood with such blunt-force trauma that to this day I am still feeling its effects.

Teenagehood is all about exploring who you are, however, it has the filter of what you have learned in your formative years. That didn't give me a lot to work with, especially regarding relationships. I did, though, further develop my cognitive skills, as well as my creative ones; skills that proved essential to my healing later on. These were probably also developed from my previous negative experiences, but in a good way. When you travel to the depths of humanity, you learn survival skills that prove indispensable. Creativity is a wonderful gift and healer from the damage caused by plunging to the depths.

I E.M.P.O.W.E.R.
HEAL KIT INITIATIVE 3
- POWER

TAKE RIGHT ACTION

~ "There's no magic self-esteem pill, no meditative practice, or willpower, or changing behaviours that will help. The only thing to improve self-esteem is to allow the 'self' to be expressed in a healthy way." ~
Deepak Chopra

WE ARE ABLE TO ADOPT CERTAIN ACTIONS TO EMPOWER OURselves and contribute greatly to our world. Whether it be in a big or small way, it is equally important. Everything we do matters; every decision, every thought, every action, and when we choose to take the RIGHT action to support our own healing, we are stepping towards our own empowerment and we are increasing our ability to help others.

True power comes from taking right action by going with that more painful, but healthier option that you know supports your healing, and from facing the consequences by letting go of something you once loved. Even in the smallest way, these decisions are the ones that fill up your spiritual bank account, and if you don't take right action, it debits the account and your self-esteem drops. What you put up with is what you end up with.

When you decide to heal and take right action to support your beliefs, you can't expect the results to be immediate either. That would be like eating badly for twenty years, going on a diet for two days, and then wondering why all the weight hasn't miraculously gone and you don't look like Channing Tatum yet. It took me a year and a half after quitting my crappy job to find my dream job. I quit my marriage and still haven't found a soul mate after four years, but I know that I will find the RIGHT person next time because I have empowered myself by taking the right actions.

WHAT DOES AN EMPOWERED PERSON LOOK LIKE?

When I think of empowered people I think of people who have made the right decisions in their lives. However, this isn't just about "powerful" people. There are plenty of powerful people who are not empowered in this sense. They get to positions of power by bullying and by making negative decisions that produce a lot of money and harm others. I am not including these people in my empowered bunch. True power is internal and it doesn't come just from good things happening to you. It comes from empowering yourself in situations that are not so great in your life. In fact, the worse the situation, the greater the opportunity for empowering yourself by taking right action.

Think of those people whom you might consider to be empowered. I think of Nelson Mandela, Viktor Frankl, Clara Hughes, and Rosa Parks. One striking thing all of these people have in common is that they have all suffered greatly and have not only overcome their traumas, but have woven them into the framework of who they are, in order that they can use them to help other people. You could almost say it is their driving force and you can see it in all the decisions they make or have made about how they live or have lived their lives. It's not just the big decisions either; often it's the smaller ones that have the most impact. Rosa Parks was tired after working hard all day and wanted to sit down on the bus. She decided not to give up her seat; a seemingly small decision with huge consequences, given the context. She took action to support her belief that she deserved better, or that she at least deserved equality. All of these empowered people accepted their realities with grace and with small decision after small decision, turned their misfortune into their platform for helping other people. These are truly empowered people. They don't just have to be people of note. I'm sure you know people in your community who carry the same weight on perhaps a smaller scale, but their character and qualities are the same. They choose the right action, not just for themselves but also for those around them. If you want to heal, then you need to adopt this healthy decision-making. However, just because you are volunteering your time, doesn't mean you are being altruistic. The power comes from your intention for the volunteer work. I sometimes challenge myself to do random acts of kindness that no one else knows about. It's the fact that no one will know that gives me the power; not the accolades from people noticing my good deeds. I would tell you about them here, but that would defeat the purpose of their anonymity, now wouldn't it? ;-)

SPIRITUAL BANKING – INTERNAL POWER

Most of us keep track of our financial banking: What goes in? What comes out? What bill can't I pay? How am I going to get to the end of the month before I come to the end of the money? Or maybe for you it's: What investments should I make? What can I do to minimise my taxes?

Whatever the case, almost everyone in the Western world has a financial bank account. What I believe is that everyone also has an emotional and spiritual bank account that we add to or take away from every day, and the outcome is that it impacts our souls, our spirits, and our beings. Yet not many people keep track of these accounts. It's amazing that something so long lasting and influential in our lives gets so little focus, especially considering that the balance of our spiritual bank accounts often define how well we manage our financial bank accounts.

My belief is that we don't actually acknowledge just how significant withdrawals and deposits in our spiritual and emotional bank accounts are in our lives. Everything we do has a consequence. Spiritually if we meditate, our emotions will be calmed. If we yell and scream at people, we will get our spiritual butts kicked eventually. What if we believed that everything we did mattered? Each seemingly small decision where we don't speak up for ourselves when we could, makes a withdrawal from our account. Every time we make those ostensibly small decisions to do what's right for us; what's in our hearts, it deposits into our account and the dividends are things like self-esteem, courage, integrity, and wholeness.

The good news is there's no overdraft on this type of account. It's an absolute that can only stay in the positive. Once you're at zero, your self-esteem may be really low, but if you just make some deposits it can soon replenish. That's exactly what I've been successfully doing. This helped create the remarkable life I am leading now. It's not so much that my life circumstances are getting better, but rather that I am making better decisions to improve my life circumstances. Each decision empowers me further, and I gain authentic power from my emotional and spiritual bank deposits.

Power cannot be gleaned from anything external like money, status, other people, or career. These are all things that can be taken away at any time. So if you are relying on these things for your power, you will be stripped bare when they change: corporate downsizing; a house fire; public scandal; or a divorce can all tear you to shreds. Internal power stays with you in times of disaster, in fact it even strengthens. When you make the tough decisions it builds you, irrespective of what is going on around you at the time. You could have nothing except your self-esteem, your integrity, and your ability to see that you are resourceful and you will figure something out to get back on track with whatever was lost. If you lose everything and have no self-esteem or integrity, then good luck trying to dig yourself out of that hole. That's when people become suicidal as hope disappears, and they have nothing to fall back on as all their power came from external things. Even in those times, though, I believe that if you then decide to take right action, you can still build yourself up again, just like I did. But before I did, I made a lot of wrong decisions that had a major impact on my life, far greater than I could have ever imagined.

THE IMPACT OF NOT TAKING RIGHT ACTION

Every day there are moments when we can choose one way or the other, and then there are moments in life that converge at a point of decision that can splinter your life off into a different direction. It's a gathering of multiple aspects of your life that unite into one moment; an informed choice, as it's the only time and place all of our threads come together at that instant. Which decision you make can have long- lasting impact, just like Rosa Parks not wanting to give up her seat. Peter's phone call was just that for me, although the impact of my decision was negative since I did not go with the decision that was best for me and others.

I was just seventeen and still living at home in Sydney, Australia. Peter's and my relationship was my first real one. We'd only been dating a short while, a few months maybe, and this was my first "please take me back" phone call ever. For me, it was the beginning of a new, self-destructive path that would be so devastating that twenty-seven years later in 2012, I would be contemplating where and when the hell my life got so screwed up. It's often the simple decisions in life that lead us in one direction or another. The bigger moments change our lives and they can come without our knowledge or consent, but they are not solely what makes up our lives. Our true resonant moments are not the big traumas, the promotions, the births, or the deaths; our lives are made up of our decisions about what we do with those events and what we do in the lead up. How we choose to react and how we decide to deal with the feelings that surface because of those events is what "life" is, and becomes. We can change the trajectory we are on by our reactions to life events, and by anticipating consequences of our current actions. *What we do today about yesterday's events, will determine what tomorrow looks like.*

Our true resonances are at that turning point after a catalyst, in which we ask the deepest part of our souls: What am I willing to do to be the best that I can be? We can choose what will benefit those around us and lead us to a healthier path, or we can choose to feel good in a moment of instant gratification. We can shut down those horrible "feelings" and smother them with food, sweep them under the carpet, drown them in alcohol, or escape them using drugs, excessive exercise, shopping, staying in abusive relationships, or whatever our "drug of choice" is. Then we end up in a toxic place; one where we are presented with different life events that have different choices attached – but we can always choose the healthier path. I don't believe there are any circumstances where we can't react to empower ourselves. Nelson Mandela reminds us that no jail cell can bind us, because a guard cannot control what you think.

Viktor Frankl, in his book *Man's Search for Meaning*, shows us that even in the concentration camps no life circumstance can necessarily prevent us from choosing how we think about what's happening. "Everything can be taken from a man but one thing: the last of the human freedoms—to choose one's attitude in any given set of circumstances, to choose one's own way."

However, at seventeen I was not that enlightened. I hadn't read Viktor Frankl yet. Teenagers have not yet developed the brain function to accurately predict a future consequence when they're faced with a decision. Adults are not always that great at it either, but teenagers don't even have the option. I could never have understood in that moment, that twenty-seven years later I'd see that this was the point at which my life seriously went off track. Not just because I stayed with Peter, which led me to the gang rape, but also because it was the first real decision I had made in a significant, intimate relationship.

It was going to colour the way I behaved in intimate relationships for many years to come. It was one of those resonant moments. Had I decided not to go out with Peter any more, it would have hurt at the time, but it would have boosted my self-esteem enough for me to say, "I am worth more than this!" It would have made a huge deposit into my spiritual bank account. Instead I chose the easy path, the one that didn't hurt at the time, which was much more immediately satisfying but led to almost deadly consequences. That's how simple it is. It wasn't some major traumatic event that led me to change my life, but rather a simple whisper suggesting that had I stood up for myself, trusted my gut instinct, and taken the right action, my life would have been so much better. My spiritual bank account would have been full and my heart would have remained open to more truly loving experiences. And in later intimate relationships I would have had better self-esteem and integrity, and so I would have chosen better people to be around. But that was not to be.

It was early on in my relationship with Peter. I was still living at home in Sydney, still at school, and like many teenagers, thinking how mature I was to have a boyfriend. But the night before, something had gone wrong. I had been summoned to be at Peter's side to bear witness to his true nature in all its glory. He was drunk, it was two a.m., and he had "parked" on the sidewalk inches away from a storefront. He was obnoxious and disrespectful, and he lured me into abandoning my values to come to his aid. I'd never been in love before, so I didn't recognise that this wasn't it. The relationship with Peter reflected the main male love of my life, which had been my abusive father, so it felt right in a way.

The scene truly shocked me. I hadn't seen this side of Peter before now. I hadn't had to face this type of scenario before, and I was really lost as to how to deal with it. Peter, seeing my hesitation, was quick to shrewdly twist and turn to manipulate me into being his "only" support. He could see that I had my running shoes on and was about to use them.

"I love you so much," were words I'd heard before, but not with all the attention that went with it. I savoured the moment, although with uncertainty, and then it happened – the deal breaker. I don't even remember what he said, but it was just…off. I felt angry but kept my cool and told him to go home. I would drive his badly parked car back to his house and walk back to my own car at two a.m. at seventeen years old. That was it for me. I was done. My naiveté didn't stretch that far to think that it was ok.

The phone call came kind of late the next day. By then I had gone through a multitude of reasoning in my head. What was I going to say? How was I going to end it? I had told my mother earlier in the day that if Peter called I didn't want to talk to him. Then as time wore on and he didn't call, I lost my passion and said, "It's ok. I can deal with him now." I'd seen a wave of relief wash over my mother when I told her things had gone off-track with Peter and I was going to end it. She was aware of what he was like.

I was still in denial. I had come to a great resolution. Proud of myself, I puttered around the house feeling almost content . . . and then he rang.

"Hi what are you doing?"…as if nothing had happened the previous night.

"Ah, nothing."

This was not the phone call I'd been expecting. I was expecting, "I love you, I screwed up, please take me back!"

I was ready with answers; direct and assertive! "How dare you do something like that to me; drag me out of bed in the middle of the night to a drunken idiot, so I have to drive your car home, and then walk back to my own car by myself at two a.m.!"

It was all sounding very reasonable in my head. Justified! Well thought-out, considering my feelings. I was not expecting, "What are you doing?" with no sign of remorse or even consciousness of the previous evening. I was dumbstruck and didn't know what to say.

"So what happened last night?" I said, hopeful for a glimmer of understanding.

"I dunno, I don't remember, I feel ok now though - must have been really drunk last night with the boys."

Perplexed, I asked, "So you have no recollection of seeing me last night?"

The conversation continued its dance, weaving and ducking for cover, all to my confused and bruised heart. At some point I realised he knew exactly what had happened, and that he'd slept it all off, realised I would be pissed, and had come up with a story that I couldn't refute. How can you argue with someone who doesn't remember?

He even said, "Well IF I did anything to upset you, I'm really sorry!"

Ha! "If!" He didn't even take a smidgen of responsibility.

Then it happened; the convergence. I felt it run through my soul. This was the moment to start a new path; which path was it going to be? I felt all my past experiences and their consequences merging – I felt the transition from girl to woman. What decision was I going to make in my present that would affect my future? Would I follow my dysfunctional relationships with men as laid down by my father, or would I sweep problems under the carpet like my mother? Would I remain strong and heal the relationship in a healthy way? I was in my last year of school, was itching to leave home, and craved a loving man. I felt grown up, even though I had no idea how immature I really was.

Peter's words drifted off. It all sounded like bullshit, but I wasn't sure. I had no yardstick with which to measure it. I asked myself what I wanted, and Peter's words turned into background noise as I reflected. Would I go to the Conservatorium of Music to do my bachelor's degree? Would I follow my mother's footsteps into nursing? Was that even what I wanted? What other fields did I want to be part of? I had always wanted to be a policewoman, but the height rules still prevented me from fostering that dream. What about a paramedic? Would being with this man facilitate that? It seemed like all my hopes and fears rolled into one second. It felt like I had an image of what my life was going to be. I saw myself twenty years from then, happy, married, maybe with children. I was laughing and life felt good. It was just a fleeting glimpse, but I knew it was possible.

Which decision in my present would lead me to this wonderful future? Was it really to be loved by this man? Was it to stand my ground? I was confused. I tuned back in to Peter. By then he had started to throw the love fest at me – a sum of his mastery in manipulation. Even though I was not consciously aware of it, I knew what he was doing in the pit of my soul. It felt wrong. I bowed my head at needing the feeling of love. No one had ever paid me so much attention. It was addicting. I had been starved of that feeling that someone wanted me. He sent me flowers with romantic notes, he touched my body like it had never been touched, and he paid attention to what I was doing. I was no longer just a background singer; I was the star, and at times, it felt awesome. Because I had no internal power, I relied on those around me to boost me up, so letting that go was too difficult for me at the time. I had also been groomed for this moment. My doting, yet abusive, father had taught me by experience. Love = Pain. When you feel like your heart is receiving that gentle stroke, it will be immediately followed by abusive behaviour that wipes out your boundaries. That was love for me! What choice did I have? My past had coloured my thinking and I didn't have the wisdom at the time to make the right decision and extract myself from the foundations laid down years before.

Then the final question: "So do you want to get together?"

My immature soul bent to the appealing sweep-it-under-the-carpet-so-I-don't-have-to-be-in-pain concept, with all its baggage and complications, and any hope of me ever living a normal happy life faded into oblivion. I had made my choice at the convergence. I had convinced myself that I was over-reacting due to my past experiences, but really I was just walking the path established by my father before Peter. It was done.

A small pain went through my physical body as I said, "Yes! Let's get together."

This is how all those years later, in 2012, I was wondering how my life got so screwed up. It was through these small moments when I could have shown my strength and instead decided to ignore my feelings and go with the drug of the day, which is what I thought was love. This is because my spiritual bank account was empty. This was not right action.

So when I got the opportunity to do it over again with my wife Angie, I didn't bow to instant gratification. I took the pain and I took my medicine and benefited markedly. We have choices like this every day. I will concede that they don't all have the devastating consequences that taking Peter back did, but they do affect our lives profoundly. These right actions mean the difference between authentic, happy, and real selves and unhappy, broken, low self-esteem selves. This is what right action provides. It is our inner power and can only be made by us. There is always a choice - even when things happen beyond our control, how we react is it's still our choice. And there is always a choice that supports our healing even if it's painful. We need to stand up for what we really believe in. I knew in my heart my decision was wrong, I just didn't know how to fight it. We can't say we hold these beliefs in high regard and then not back them up with action. If we do, they are just fantasy and not beliefs at all.

TAKE RIGHT ACTION WHEN EMOTION OVERWHELMS

~ "Between stimulus and response there is a space. In that space is our power to choose our response. In our response lies our growth and our freedom." ~ **Viktor Frankl**

IT'S ALL WELL AND GOOD TO REVIEW OUR OPTIONS AT A POINT of decision to go this way or that. Sometimes, though, it's not so much a decision as it is a confrontation. Emotion is our natural regulator, and most of the time we are prewired for our emotional responses to stimuli created by our previous decision-making and experiences. However, in the space between a stimulus and response is a choice in how we deal with the emotions that arise. Some say that the size of that space between the two is our maturity level. Either way, it is a pathway to use mindfulness to observe what is coming up, and we can then take right action to empower our next step. In later chapters I discuss how to rewire the responses, but here I am addressing what to do once those reactions arise.

Having PTSD means that you can get overwhelmed with seemingly insignificant stimuli that is somehow a reminder of the traumatic event. Every time I get a pap smear test, I cry uncontrollably and feel sick. Consequently, I haven't had one in about six years; which is understandable given my history. Now I don't think I will ever have a different response, unless under sedation, and even with that I still cry. Often, there will be some behaviours around trauma that never change. You can desensitise up to a point, but some reactions, like mine to my pap smear, don't change much. Still, there are some reactions, even severe ones, that you do have control over. To minimise the rage that naturally occurs as a result of trauma, you can redirect it towards a single-minded physical and mental goal with a meditative quality, and over time the rage will lessen, as will the overwhelming emotions.

I am not a runner. There are too many body parts that fly in opposite directions, but I enjoy running. I tried doing it a few times a week, but after a while it lost its appeal as I didn't have a goal to move towards. At that stage I was going to a gym on a regular basis, as Vancouver winters are not conducive to healthy outdoor running. I had befriended this amazing lady, who at fifty-six had already completed seventy Ironman championships, while her husband was coming up to his 200th. She is the only woman to ever complete all Ironman events on every continent. She encouraged me so much that she convinced me to go on a "little run," one that for her was a warm-up to a proper run. We went in the 10km *Vancouver Sun* Run together, although I use the term "together" loosely as we started together but within five seconds Elizabeth had taken off into the distance. She did wait for me at the end as I came in forty-five minutes later. It took me an hour and a half. I was so slow that both a grandma and a seven-year-old passed me…but I finished. Every muscle ached and even my feet hurt, but I was so happy to have pushed myself beyond what I thought I could do. Even in training, every time I ran, I used it to positively reinforce my self-worth and I pushed myself to keep going. There were days I didn't feel like it, but by using TIEWIN, I accepted whatever I could do that day as long as I was out there. Fast and slow walking, running, run-walking, whatever it was I could do that day I congratulated myself for, and over time, a 10km run seemed achievable. No judgement was allowed.

PHOTO: My friend Elizabeth Model – the only woman up to 2016 who has completed every Ironman triathlon race on the planet. She joins an elite bunch who has achieved the same, one of whom is her husband John Wragg, who has completed more than 200 Ironman triathlons. Elizabeth is an elite athlete, who encouraged this chubby, slow person at the gym with as much enthusiasm as if I was at her level – a wonderful supporter.

A side note is that I was forty-six when I ran this race, and my finish time was 1:27. Interesting, given that the number I was given was determined well before the race. I just take it as a sign that it was meant to be.

I employed TIEWIN to know that when I was out there, even if I just did twenty minutes, that would be exactly what I needed that day. I ran mindfully and acknowledged every step as a step towards my healing even if it was just a walk. I employed others to support my healthy choices and Elizabeth was my cheerleader and in my corner, (which you will read about in the next chapter). I wouldn't have done the fun run without her, and the empowerment I felt from achieving the goal and pushing myself physically beyond what I thought I could, greatly reduced some of the rage from the trauma and helped me through those days I wasn't feeling that good emotionally. I found I could breathe through my body while running and it would somehow dissipate the depression and rage. At times on the pavement, each step became quite rhythmic; this was my meditation. I find that when I am emotional, I can't sit still and meditate, but this was effective. Just being mindful of the rhythm of my steps was helpful and calmed me considerably. I may not have been able to interrupt a crisis, but over the period of my months of training, the number of moments during which I became overwhelmed by emotion from the same stimulus dropped by at least half. I could even deliberately think about that which upset me the most while running and allow it to pulse through me, and it dissipated.

The fact that I had a goal to work towards meant that at the point of decision, when I really didn't feel like running though I knew it would benefit me, it made it easier to get out there and overcome the resistance. And the fact that I didn't berate myself if I could only do twenty minutes gave me even more motivation. Whatever the goal - it has to push you beyond what you think you can do. Staying safe doesn't do anything to promote healing. It has to somehow physically allow the release of intense emotion. Some people choose knitting a sweater, some people ride bikes, or climb a mountain. For me I just did a 10km run. Once I'd achieved that goal, I moved on to something else challenging. Physically I wasn't capable of doing a half-marathon, but I did go climbing regularly and went to a spin class where my goal was to keep up with the class. That was all I needed to keep pushing and challenging myself, and also to disperse the energy of emotional build up.

Climbing is a perfect activity for PTSD sufferers, as you set small goals for yourself and achieve them, and that builds your confidence as a climber. Then you move to a harder goal and so on. How you approach the rock or wall is very indicative of how you are approaching your life at that moment. I often sit around the gym waiting for my muscles to get the blood back in them, and I watch how people approach their climbs. Some sit back and say, "I can't do that," without even giving it a go. When I find myself doing that I check my attitude and at least try it before claiming that "I can't." More often than not, I actually can! It's so reflective of how I approach my life. When I find myself saying, "I can't," even before I attempt it, I now catch myself and change my attitude.

PHOTO: Me climbing – taking a breather to figure out how I'm going to get over the obstacle ahead, metaphorically and literally speaking. Forty-seven years old. It's never too late to start something new. I love it so much.

So that's long term, but sometimes you need immediate assistance. Sometimes you will be triggered by a stimulus and you don't want to react badly. The best thing I found is putting as much space between the stimulus and your external response as possible. You won't be able to control the internal response, but knowing that will help you understand that you only need to manage your outburst for fifteen seconds. Fifteen seconds is about how long it takes for the immediate rush to pass. Now anyone can control his or her outburst for fifteen seconds. You need to find something that allows you to acknowledge your response without bursting out and yelling at the kids, or screaming at your partner, or yelling at the traffic. You may find something physical helps; a deep exhale that forces all the air from your lungs; a push-up or star jump; or something silent that interrupts the flow of the response, like a word that boots you off your course. I use the word Foxtrot. It's sharp and it feels like swearing but isn't. Find your interrupter.

Once you have "interrupted" the emotional intensity, you can ground yourself in an emotional way by acknowledging that what you are feeling has NOTHING to do with your current situation. It's just that it has triggered the pain in you. Once you disconnect your reaction with your present situation, you can then go about your business of acknowledging your pain (as in Initiative 2 mindfulness).

If your stimulus is a trigger that will put you into a major flashback, then find ways to ground yourself physically in the present and acknowledge that you are safe in the immediate circumstance. This is like my pap smear; there are no ways I can interrupt the flow of emotion that goes with my pap smear, as it's too close a trigger to the original stimulus. But I can still live a normal life. I ask the doctor for Valium before I go, and I also use breathing techniques to help me accept my reality that I am safe despite what my emotions are telling me. It's ok to react in this circumstance, and sometimes just knowing that I will react, allows me to express it and move through it more quickly. When the immediate trigger hits the fan, I breathe and for the thirty seconds of smearing I ride the wave of emotion without acting on it. And as soon as we are done, I find that I can get back to normal fairly quickly. A few minutes later, all the fear is gone. Now that would be different if I engaged myself in my reaction and believed that my life was in danger. Instead, I focus on my present moment of safety.

Getting a pap smear is not something I can avoid, unless I put my life in danger. If I was attacked by a shark, I could easily avoid swimming, as it's not imperative to regular life, but avoidance generally gets worse over time. For instance, if you have a car accident, you might tense up at that intersection, but if you avoid it, it will translate to all intersections and soon all roads, and then soon you won't be able to drive or even walk near a road. So it's better to desensitise yourself as best you can; to jump in knowing that a reaction is coming is good. Use mindfulness to feel what's in the space between the stimulus and the response. A focus on breathing is a really effective calming tool.

So having decided this, I was brave and went and got my pap smear after several years, even without Valium. I freaked out, but I breathed through it and survived. It shouldn't be such a big deal next time.

My doctor helped me through the reaction. She has a good sense of humour, and I find that helpful. She said, "I'm guessing that you don't want the student doctor in here," as she brought in this pimply-faced, geeky-looking kid.

I said, "Ah no!"

And then after she finished she said, "I forgot to take your blood pressure earlier, can I get that quickly?"

I laughed and said, "You're kidding right?"

She took my pressure and it was through the roof. "Maybe we'll get your pressure next time," she said.

Just remember it's ok to be reactive without engaging. TIEWIN! Now, my next challenge. . .the dentist! Lol! It's been around a seven-year hiatus for that.

TAKING RESPONSIBILITY

~ "One's philosophy is not best expressed in words; it is expressed in the choices one makes...and the choices we make are ultimately our responsibility." ~ **Eleanor Roosevelt**

TO FURTHER EMPOWER YOUR CHOICES THAT ARE NECESSARY TO heal from whatever ails you, is taking responsibility. This doesn't mean you caused the terrible events in your life, but how you react to such events is your responsibility. If you make bad choices because you have a negative reaction, that is totally your responsibility. The sooner we realise our power in this initiative, the sooner we can make lasting change in our lives in the way we react and the subsequent outcomes.

In 2013, a couple of years after I had moved to Vancouver, I chose to no longer fight against my reality even though I was about to lose my house back in Montreal. I hated my job because it made me surrender my personal values every day. I also had broken many valuable relationships. I had disconnected from my family and my ability to connect to my wife at a deep level had a big trust issue in front of it. I had anxiety and depression much of my week despite taking every prescription drug and vitamin under the sun to try to rectify that. My stepdad was dying and my finances weren't recovering under the circumstances at the time. Losing my house might have meant I wouldn't get my Canadian citizenship, but here's the thing with all that. . . Fighting against it would have hurt me more and for longer than if I just surrendered to it, or even welcomed it. Those circumstances may not have been my fault, but it was my responsibility to take care of them as best I could. Fighting against my reality was wasted energy that could have been put to better use in healing. If I thought that healing was about getting all my ducks in a row with my career, finances, friends, etc. then I was fighting the wrong battle. This was an inner battle not an outer one.

PHOTO: *My little house in Montreal, Quebec, circa 2008. It comes complete with pussycat in the window and doggie at the front door.*

THE HOUSE ALBATROSS

I had moved from Australia to Montreal, Canada in 2005. My intention was to work, travel, and see how I liked it. I had been at the same company for seven years and I guess I had started to get the seven-year itch. I was lucky in that the company I worked for had a subsidiary company in Canada, so I moved there with the same job, the same pay, and the same company structure. I LOVED Canada so much that I decided to stay. In 2008, I was finally in a position where I had a steady job, good pay, and good friends, and I really wanted to grow up a little more and purchase my own house. I had just received a substantial payout for victim's compensation for the crimes committed against me twenty-something years before and I used that for a down-payment on a house.

I loved my little house so much. It was me. I could do anything; plant a flower, paint a room, sing, get a dog, and pay off my own space rather than give out dead rent money. But when I lost my job and had difficulty speaking the French language well enough to get another job, despite my efforts, I had to move on. I moved to Ottawa for work and was hoping to eventually move back to Montreal to my little house, but it wasn't to be so. I could have sold it then, but it was so cute I wanted to hold on a little longer, so I rented it out.

Being a landlord in a different province and not really knowing the Quebec rules for tenancy became a nightmare. After a year and a half of unruly tenants, I tried to sell the house, to no avail. The house eventually became my albatross; a heavy weight around my neck that never went away. In reality I had many opportunities to choose differently, but for whatever reason I didn't apply them at the time. The first time I put the house on the market I got an offer the next day. Of course I didn't accept it as I was trying to get more money to be able to get myself out of debt, and hold onto my victim's compensation money. Of course no other offers came forward after that. By the second time I put it on the market I was already screwed. Tenants had left the place in a mess, they hadn't taken care of it as I had, and the market had crashed. So then into my third time it was pretty much the last chance. Even though I was suffering greatly for it at that moment, I also acknowledged that it was my own bad decision-making that had gotten me there. I could have taken the first and only offer as the house had already caused me enough grief. I'd have walked away with some debt, but it would have been manageable and I wouldn't have had house stress from trying to rent or sell while living in a different province.

Not only that, I had plenty of opportunity to sell the house while I was still in it, after I decided to move cities to get work in Ottawa. I could have easily put it on the market, but that was more of an emotional decision due to the fact that I couldn't let go of my beautiful little house that I loved so much. It made me feel so good, it was mine, I could express myself any way I wanted to, and it was the first time I had my own space. Eventually I wanted to move back to Montreal too. There was a unique freedom with my house that I had never experienced, which is ironic given the bind I then found myself in where it was drowning me. The story of my life; I find something really good and I can't have it for whatever reason or I sabotage it somehow. It's also a common theme for me to hold onto something longer than its usefulness, even at my own risk and harm. Even if it was suitable at one time it, I found it really difficult to let go of what was not working anymore. I had great fears over losing stuff that felt good. It's that letting go of the 50% satisfaction to go to 0%, rather than realising that holding onto 50% not only had great negative ramifications but also prevented the 90% of good stuff from coming into my life.

The relationship with my house was no longer working. My French wasn't strong enough to reside in Quebec, and although Ottawa was great, it wasn't a city I wanted to stay in long term. My wife, whom I'd met in Ottawa, and I had decided to move way over to the other side of the country to Vancouver, BC, so the real estate that was difficult to manage from afar became much, much, more difficult from 5000kms away. It was this kind of truth that I dodged; that I hid from myself at weaker times due to the pain it would cause if I allowed myself to realise it. But the pain of holding onto an illusion was far more damaging. I could have lost everything, all to maintain my illusion of peace. Even so it's really hard to let go sometimes, even knowing how much damage your decisions are creating. But there's always a point where a choice is made. Do I go with what I know to be truly healing or do I continue my destructive path?

This time, I chose healing, but some of the damage had already been done. After years of pain of suffering and trying to sell my house and trying to get my rent, I stepped into the void and let go. I had recently left my wife by this stage and was already in a tailspin, which as I've mentioned is often a good place to be as you are much more real and more likely to make the tougher decisions. All the niceties are stripped away and you can see your life much more clearly. I accepted my reality and my responsibility, and I foreclosed on the house and went bankrupt; all because I stayed in denial and couldn't face a little pain over losing the house after its usefulness was done. It was a heavy price to pay. My credit will be shot until at least 2020, which affects my ability to change jobs to a police force. Even moving house could prove difficult in setting up electricity, or Internet or anything that requires a credit history. It affects everything. Vancouver is not the easiest city to live in and competing for rental properties is hard enough without a big bankruptcy in front of it.

Having said that though, at least I didn't feel like a victim in that moment because it really was my own stupid choices that led me there. I knew why I was there. I had opportunity after opportunity to sell the house, but I didn't. There was peace in knowing that it was my own decisions that had led me to be in that position. What I needed to do was make sure I was totally real with myself from that point forward with any part of my life, so that I didn't make the same negative decisions again. It's easy to tell if I'm not living truthfully when I am mindful. I realise that I have been overeating, I feel tension in my body where it shouldn't be, I make rash decisions, and I feel depressed. My own ignorance plays a huge part in my depression and anxiety, and if I'm totally real – then the lesson will not be lost, and my suffering will have served some purpose. The universe is like that. It will send us those little whispers that you hear with your inner voice and if you don't listen, it smacks you in the head! (Ok, there's a few steps between those two but you get the picture.)

Amazingly enough, even though I was in that situation of losing my financial stability; the house, and I was still recovering from leaving Angie, I felt calm and relaxed. That is what I wished for myself from that point forward: Peace. However, you can't expect to make hard decisions and expect life will run smoothly. Peace must be earned, and when you step forward into healing, friends, family, circumstances, and the universe will tug you back just to push you to ask, "Have you really changed? Or is this new responsibility a passing phase?" It's like the plateau you hit after exercising for a while. You lose weight and get fit initially, and then it slows down a little. That's where the true test is. Are you willing to keep going even when it seems like you're not getting where you want? "What are you willing to do to be the best version of yourself?"

STANDING UP - THE FIRE

So I'd lost my wife, my house, and my financial stability, but at least I had a job in Vancouver. I didn't like the job I had, but at least I had one.

"Today in the news, firemen from three cities are fighting a blaze after a huge explosion in. . . [the city where I worked]."

Hmmm! I don't know the street they're talking about. I'd better look it up on Google to see if traffic will be affected in the . . . "Oh shit! That's my block!"

The city block of about six buildings where I worked was up in flames. It appeared through the plumes of smoke that my office was still standing, although I wasn't sure. All of those buildings were connected, so it was hard to distinguish where one ended and the next one began.

After frantic, six a.m. calls to my boss, my instructors who were teaching that day at the first aid centre, and my admin staff, I made my way down to the scene. Nervous about the thirty bottles of oxygen stored in the classrooms, I immediately made my way to the fire chief and reported the contents of my building. As things came to mind that I had to take care of, I called my boss and updated her on the fire status. I asked her to take care of everything as it came to mind, as I didn't have access to my computer or calendar or contacts, for obvious reasons. Her response was less than helpful. There I was standing in front of the second biggest fire in the city's history, watching the block where I worked have water pouring out of it from the fire fighters' efforts. The buildings next to mine were being levelled by a bulldozer in efforts to keep the intact buildings from catching fire. And my boss said, "You know, one phone call would have sufficed, not three! You should have thought of everything before calling me."

I was taken aback. I would have expected from a non-profit community-based organisation that they would have been compassionate and caring about the community. I was expecting, *Is everyone ok? Can we do anything to help?* This totally incongruous reaction was the last straw for me. My bully boss had harassed me enough and I wasn't going to take it anymore. This wasn't our first incident. I had been harassed by this woman all year, mostly over things that were out of my control.

I met up with one of my friends, Bill, who was about to lose everything. His father had started the sign business in 1949 in this city, and all of his memorabilia from his dad was still in the office. Not only that, his dad painted most of the signage in the city block that was now being razed to the ground.

The fire was finally controlled and Bill's shop was the first one on the block still standing – hugely damaged but still standing. Mine was next to his on the upright side so it was fine, but over forty businesses had lost it all. No one was going to be allowed back into the buildings for some time while city assessors and engineers evaluated the damage.

Bill was devastated. He had watched the fire in the morning on the news, sitting next to his dad, who now had Alzheimer's and didn't really understand what was going on, although he cried at the sight of the fire devouring his former livelihood. I told Bill to look at the bright side. At least with Alzheimer's his dad wouldn't remember it tomorrow.

Bill said, "But I will."

I gave him a big hug.

Our connection was interrupted by a phone call from my boss asking me when I could make it to one of the other branches to do some work as, "I'm not paying you to stand around the streets all day."

That was it for me. A boundary had been crossed that was irreversible. I realised I was in the wrong place for work. Once again, it's not like I didn't know that already, but I hadn't accepted until then the reality that if I wanted to heal, I had to leave. The right action was to find another job and not overstep my values every day. I had to stand up for my beliefs and make sure they weren't just fantasies. I hadn't accepted just how much the work situation was affecting my self worth at the time, but everything you do, think, and say matters.

Sometimes there are moments that resonate through your whole life. Sometimes you have to be willing to risk it all to take a stand on something you believe in. This was one of those moments. I had to be willing to walk away from something I'd put my time and energy and life into, and which I had wanted so badly that it almost physically hurt to think of leaving it behind. Yet that's what I needed to do if I really wanted to take a stand. I was about to lose my job, my ability to pay my bills, perhaps lose my beautiful paradise on the North Shore along everything I had worked for over the last few years, to stand up to a bully. All after already losing so much.

Just because it was the right thing to do and was very healing to finally stand up to a bully boss, didn't mean it wouldn't cost anything. In fact, truly healing means that you have to lay everything on the line and be willing to let go of it all. Ellen DeGeneres stepped into the void to come out as gay. She lost her TV show, her money, her friends, and a whole host of other things, but she did not lose her dignity or integrity, and look at her now. Rosa Parks risked her life when she refused to give up her seat on the bus to a white person. Oddly enough she died on October 24th, 2005. The day I wrote this was eight years later to the day of her death, and as I typed this from my handwritten notes, it was December 1st, 2013, Rosa Parks Day - the day she was arrested. (This is by coincidence only, although I don't believe in coincidence.)

It is possible to be who you are in the face of everyone telling you it's a bad idea. I was being told I was stupid to let go of one job before I had another, but I knew for myself what was right for me. No one else had the full picture. I was willing to step into the void too, but it's hard to walk out of a job to go to nothing. I was completely exhausted and needed recuperation. I had stayed in that horrible job way beyond my own capacity to cope with it. I had stayed in a marriage well beyond what I had to give and I held onto a house that had long since lost its value to me. Had I listened and been mindful earlier about all of these things, I wouldn't have been forced into this position, but once I was in it, I had to act rightly. I had to quit.

To choose something like this is true power. It may not feel like it at the time, but the ripples of choosing this action are far greater than staying in a job I hated with values that made me cringe. It took a couple of years to get back on track, but the job I landed sometime later is the same one I am in now and it's fantastic. From a TIEWIN perspective, had I not stood up for myself and left my job when I did, I wouldn't have found this awesome job I am in now. What if I had stayed, which historically was my tendency to do? Two years later I still would have been fighting the same fights with the bully boss, I would have had no self-esteem, and I would have been deeply unhappy and depressed. Once I stepped into the void and allowed myself some recovery time, I chose an easy job that I could do even though I knew it wasn't for me. After a year of that, I moved on to what I really liked; managing a team of customer-service agents for a wholesale furniture store. And as I grew in self-esteem and worth, so did my job and responsibilities grow. I empowered myself to get where I needed to be. I risked everything to act rightly. And I took responsibility for all of my actions and outcomes.

PHOTO: New Westminster fire Oct 2013. The first building you see on the left is where I worked. The buildings beyond the second tree on the left were all demolished by this stage.

Young Adulthood - Missteps

SOME THINGS WERE STARTING TO BUILD AND I WAS COMING into my own. The transition from high school to the rest of my life was coming up fast and I was doing well in school. I was feeling like a grownup. I had planned to go to the Conservatorium of Music and get a music degree and perhaps teach. My music teachers were helping me get ready for the auditions and exams. I didn't even question my choice and didn't look into what I really wanted to do. This was just an assumption from my excellence in music as a whole. Unfortunately, there was a major flaw that didn't appear until it was too late. This was back in the day before school counsellors would counsel you and test you on what your skills were and help you decide what was best for you when you left school. So I actually didn't research what the minimum requirements were. I had assumed I was good at school so I would get in. When I did the entrance exam, though, I realised that I hadn't taken the right math course and it made me ineligible. I stood on the grounds of the Sydney's Conservatorium of Music, the place where I had assumed I was going to be for the next four years and realised I couldn't go there. It was a rude awakening. So I had two choices: go back to school and do the correct courses or choose something else entirely.

Once again, I didn't stop to figure out what I could do or what I wanted to do, I just reared ahead into repeating my last year of school, but at a college so I had more flexibility. Then I could get back on track and go back to "The Con," as it was known. The best-laid plans don't account for what comes up in the meantime. About halfway through the year I realised that I'd never wanted to do music as a career in the first place. I didn't know what I wanted to do, but I knew that being a music teacher wasn't it.

I searched around for what I thought I might love to do and my creativity was still at the forefront. When I saw an ad for a university course in acting, I thought I would love to do that, although it was 2500kms north in Far North Queensland. I didn't really have a good connection with my family at that stage, and moving that far didn't really phase me. So that's what I chose. Acting became my new love and I was very happy doing the course. Halfway through, though, I changed focus and studied to become a theatre director instead. I had a great mentor in the professor who ran the course, and I found that I really loved directing and was good at it. One of my best skills to this day is getting the best out of people and pushing them beyond what they think they can do. I excelled at this, which in a theatre environment made for some powerful moments. I was very creative and in a directing capacity was able to produce some commanding work.

Relationship-wise, while still at school at seventeen, I had found my salvation in Peter. He was mesmerising and the love I had craved since I'd lost my father's connection made me giddy. I was addicted to it. I moved out of home to live with him, and my life's truly destructive path took hold. The duality that existed in my whole history was still there. I achieved amazing personal goals while my relationships disassembled around me. It was subtle at first. Peter would test me and if I failed he would withdraw, which for me was unbearable as I'd almost cut off from my family and friends. I often underwent the *you don't love me enough* test, where I had to comply with whatever crazy idea of the day was. It started small with things like waiting for him for two hours after he was supposed to pick me up, while he was at the pub with his buddies. Somehow that sort of thing turned around, so it became my fault that I would complain and not be patient. Peter had his own set of rules, and because I was completely co-dependent by this stage I complied willingly but uncomfortably. At this point in my life I was the epitome of co-dependence, not just because I displayed the symptoms of what to look for in a co-dependent relationship, but also because I had the textbook history of someone who was co-dependent. At seventeen I had very little chance to be anything but who I was at the time, making it excessively difficult to break from Peter's grasp.

Eventually the rules included, *I don't love him enough because...*: I wouldn't perform sexual favours on request, or I didn't want him sleeping with his previous girlfriends. The list got bigger and bolder as we went along, and I got smaller. My voice dimmed to a whisper. At this time being "happy" on the outside was harder, but I did have some solace in my creativity and my volunteer passions. Personally, I was now just angry and depressed. However, had you asked me at the time how I felt, my perception would have been that I loved Peter dearly and he loved me. There was no mindfulness at all. I would have done almost anything for him. He isolated me from friends so that I had no other support. You might think I would have noticed it, but he was so manipulative he would make it sound like if I didn't comply then it was me who had the issue, not him.

How could my clouded judgement built around years of abuse from my father help me? I had never learned appropriate boundaries. My mom was running around after my stepdad like he was God. What hope did I have? I was the co-dependent poster child.

I did all the regular young adult things; went to university and worked during the holidays so I could help fund my year, but my friends diminished. I only had access to those I was "allowed." In other words, those who could also be controlled and manipulated by Peter. He followed me from Sydney to Townsville in North Queensland where I did my bachelor's degree. Despite all this, I did well in my studies as usual. I enjoyed university even though I was an emotional mess. I'm sure I was very challenging to be around during that time. It was very confusing.

Eventually the *you don't love me* test started to wear thin with me. I was growing up. I was moving into adulthood, crossing the teen threshold and really starting to get my own thinking going. I wasn't as easily manipulated, so the effectiveness of *you don't love me* faded.

So then it got more serious. Subtle threats of violence started to emerge. Peter would stab something like a phone book and say, "Once this Ghurkha knife is unsheathed, it has to draw blood." There was a new set of rules; much more sinister. In addition, my strength had worn down. I started to dissociate more from my life, so actually in some ways I became more pliable. I didn't care as much about what happened to me. I was now so vulnerable to being taken advantage of, anything could happen.

And unfortunately it did.

THE WORST DAY OF MY LIFE

IT WAS DURING ONE OF THE END-OF-YEAR BREAKS FROM UNIVERsity between my second and third year. Peter and I had returned to Sydney to find work and build up the finances before going back to university poor-student lifestyle. During the summer, we worked at a fish and chip shop owned by an old buddy of Peter's. All was great. Summer was hot, and money was coming in. Days were long but fun, even though the shop was greasy and hot. . . that is until Simon arrived and became the new manager. All hell broke loose then.

I had first met Simon years before as an innocent fifteen-year-old, on the beach a few hundred meters away from the fish shop. He was creepy back then and almost five years later, my older self felt even more uneasy.

The police report read, "Aggravated Sexual Assault." The difference between "aggravated" sexual assault and just plain old sexual assault is the number of people involved, and the severity of the injuries. You need at least three people for an aggravated classification. I counted at least eight, and then I stopped counting. When you think of aggravated sexual assault nothing good comes to mind, but also stereotypes arise, like being threatened with a gun or a knife at your throat to force you into doing unspeakable things. The assault on me was nothing like that. My perpetrators had a much more effective weapon; a weapon more powerful and brutal than any knife or gun – emotional weakness. They had a helpless, already abused victim, who was submissive, vulnerable, and malleable. They knew this, as the main perpetrators were my boss Simon and my boyfriend at the time, Peter. One had a position of perceived power and the other I was totally co-dependent upon.

Peter was well versed in my self-esteem inadequacies. At this stage, after four years of being together, he hardly had to utter a word and I would submit at a mere look of control. He'd already satisfied his many sexually deviant fantasies using me as the star, and I, not so willingly, had complied. I often fought, but Peter was a master manipulator, who had a blank victim's canvas to work with; to shape into whatever he fancied. Threesomes, foursomes, whateversomes. Don't get me wrong. I don't have anything against swingers; I don't find it immoral or disgusting UNLESS not everyone involved wants to participate. I have no issues with the lifestyle except for the fact that it's just not for me; it never was, and never will be. What's disgusting for me is that I was coerced, manipulated, and threatened into participating, and I feel so ashamed that I endured it, that no amount of counselling has ever been able to free me of that shame. It's very hard to rid yourself of something that you believe you deserve – no matter how illogical it seems.

I ALWAYS fell for the stories of, "We're just going to dinner with these new friends at their house," and when I resisted I would be thrown the *you don't love me* line or whatever my vulnerability of the day was. "You don't love me" doesn't sound that threatening. Most people would say, "You're right- if you ask me to do that – I don't love you!" But for me, my whole world was intertwined with Peter's. I couldn't tell what was my own thought or what was what I thought he wanted me to think. I believed I would die without him, and I just may have. I was the perfectly groomed victim. With the life I'd had, how would I know that there was more to life than this? You don't have to have life threatening trauma like I did to be totally co-dependent; you just have to be ignorant or naive about life, which can come about easily through the main people in your world and how they treated you. Did they "groom" you for success and to find your true path – or did they have their own agendas? Either way I was groomed for the latter.

Sometimes I did fight back – with dire consequences. My life would be threatened and there was a myriad of weaponry around the house to do the job. A 303 rifle used in the First World War hung on the wall, along with Japanese swords, a Gurkha knife that supposedly must draw blood if it's unsheathed, (according to Peter) a live grenade, and various other guns. Or there were the "accidents" like, "Oh, did that hurt when I jumped on your neck from a great height while you were sitting on the floor and your spine almost popped out of its skin? Oh geez, I'm sorry!"

It sounds so dumb to me now, as I'm sure it does to many of you reading this. I can hear the "Why didn't you just walk out the door?" remarks now. Believe me, I've asked myself the same question many times. There were no chains holding me down; no locks and no bars. I was free to go at any time. But by that time I had endured so much abuse that it didn't even cross my mind that leaving was an option.

Jaycee Dugard, who was kidnapped at age eleven and held captive for eighteen years, did not have chains on the door either after a while. She had free options to leave the backyard she grew up in, but she never left. She didn't know how. I can understand why. I grew up being groomed to know where the boundaries were. They weren't logical, they weren't rational, and they were not based on what we know as healthy boundaries. They were almost completely reversed. But what you learn is what you follow until you have enough maturity to question it. When I met Peter I thought I knew the world. I was intelligent, inquisitive, and courageous, but I had never had the opportunity to grow with nurturing, with love, and with all the things we need to develop healthy boundaries. Still I hear echoes of doubt about that theory. I hear the "Yeah but. . ." and to those doubts I say, "No one would knowingly choose to be abused. If they knew better, they wouldn't have chosen that path."

Simon was a man I'd met many years before when he was my boss at a beach kiosk that sold food and ice cream to hungry beachgoers. He was an asshole then and proved to only enhance those traits with age. I dreaded the day that these two dark forces, Simon and Peter, would meet and share in exploiting my vulnerabilities to catalyze a master plan of destruction that would last the rest of my life.

Schedules were ruined, pay was lowered, the fun was gone, and this guy made my skin crawl. The worst part was, Peter was becoming closer to Simon every day. They laughed about me, and they became best buds overnight. Like attracts like I guess. Either way it proved disastrous for me.

It started out as a regular day. Peter wasn't working that day. I had to take the day's takings upstairs to the apartment above the fish shop. I was looking forward to going home and relaxing after another shitty day under Simon's thumb. My intentions were to hand over the day's receipts and leave immediately, but it seemed Simon had other ideas. He directed me to come in and stay for a while. I knew something was up as soon as I saw his weird smile. He didn't smile often, so when he did it was always off-putting. It was creepy.

I said I wanted to go home, but Simon said Peter was coming over soon so I should stay. I did, but as I walked into the living room, I saw there were five young men sitting on two L-shaped sofas. They all had nothing on but running shorts and their genitals were all hanging out the sides with their legs wide open. It looked like Simon was the puppet master and we were all young and stupid and being heavily manipulated. The five guys were just like me, about eighteen or nineteen years old, fresh-faced, and looking to Simon for guidance. The sight was very confronting. I froze. I didn't know what to do or say. So I did and said nothing. My mouth was dry, I couldn't speak, I couldn't even think straight. A million things rushed through my head as I stood in shock. Simon paraded me around the room directing the young men to grope me and grab me. He told them to "Grab her ass, stick your fingers up her." He encouraged mob mentality and once it takes hold, it's very difficult to stop.

I went through a journey of my own. Was this real? What was going on? Was I dreaming? I hoped to God that I was, but unfortunately reality lay gently over me. I had a recall moment from the previous week where Peter and I had fought over just this scenario.

"It will be fun," he said.

"Over my dead body," I said...and it was nearly just that.

The cold, hard, tiled floor of the freezer room in the fish shop where I regained consciousness after we fought suddenly came back to me in full strength. But it was too late. My fate was sealed with an agreement between my deplorable boss and my abhorrent boyfriend. Simon was relishing the moment. I could see he enjoyed the control, the power, the dominance. After all, rape is not about sex, it's about control, power, and dominance.

After the staged parade, I was led toward the bedroom, or more like pulled. I discerned an opportunity for me to escape. The bedroom door was right beside the front door. My heart pounded. I was closest to the door. All I had to do was open it and run out. Simon would be powerless to stop me once I passed the threshold of the door. I stared at the lock for what seemed like an eternity. *What do I do? What if it's dead-bolted and then I get in trouble for trying to run?* When my father caught us trying to run, he would shoot at us or beat us. He would make us hold out our hands and receive beatings until we didn't flinch anymore. I learned how to be *silent* in the face of extreme danger. Even so, had I known then what I know now, I would have crashed through the door myself and screamed blue murder until someone called the police. But I didn't know – I didn't do anything and the moment, which was only a second or two, crept away. It would be my last real chance to escape and I missed it. My heart had whispered *Run!* and I had ignored it once again.

Once in the bedroom, the menacing Simon, whom I knew well, stood over me. Reality gripped me as I started to cry and beg for my release. That only spurred Simon on further. He was aggressive and directive, and I knew I could not fight such an opponent. He was forty-something. He may have been forty-three and half years old by then. His wits were more advanced than mine, or that's what I thought. Now my forty-three-and-a-half-year-old mind could stand up to someone like that. But then I was only nineteen with many vulnerabilities, and Simon knew every single one of them. He threw me on the bed after stripping me bare and said, "Lie there and shut up! Stop complaining. They all complain, No! No! When really they mean Yes! Yes!"

I knew in my heart I was about to be raped. But by whom? Simon was gay, I thought. How many? All of them? Surely not. Surely it would just be one and the others would just watch? I was shut down with fear. I could barely breathe now.

Simon reflected the same, *Stop crying or I'll give you something to cry about!* phrase that my father used to say. I felt just like I did when I was a little girl about to be hit by Dad. I may as well have been three years old, as I had just as little power over the situation.

I lay on the bed; no pillows that I can remember, no covers, just an under-sheet. Simon returned to the living room and locked the bedroom door. Then they all came in naked except Simon. I guess he wanted to remain in control at all times. He would say things like, "This is a game, she's playing a role of a prostitute, she's going to school for acting."

Well that part was true. I was on vacation from my university studies in theatre. I always worked during the summer. I was in acting school, but this was no game – my tears were real. Simon had made the perfect setup. The more I resisted, the more it resonated with the "role play" theme. So it didn't matter what I said. "No!" would always be translated into "Yes!" Simon had convinced them by having them talk to my boyfriend, who had confirmed that I was in on it and everything was fine. They'd been told Peter would be there later to celebrate with a few beers.

The boys were tentative at first. The first one got on top of me and hesitated. Simon said, "Come on fuck her!" He riled up the boys like a football team. He sounded just like a coach: "Come on! Get it in! Fuck her!" The boys soon followed the energy. They weren't even clean; it had been a hot summer's day and most of them had obviously been at the beach across the street. They smelled like sweaty ocean water. Sand. Salt. Sweat. Yuck. It wasn't like I was any picnic either, I had the grease and sweat from a day at the fish shop.

Where had Simon gotten these guys? Did he pay them? Did they pay him? They didn't seem like people he'd hang out with. They were just a group of guys; friends I think. Each one lay on top of me. It hurt every time. I tried to relax but couldn't, so it hurt me even more. I lost track of what was happening from that point on. It was hard to comprehend. My body was being pulled this way and that. At times my arms were pinned down, as were my legs. Rape. One after another. Due to Simon's "convincing" role-play justification, I'm not sure that they knew consciously what they were doing. But deep down inside they understood it was wrong. They had to know a woman wouldn't want to participate in that. Just curious boys. Always wanting to push buttons to find out what they did. Never even contemplating the consequences of their actions. For many years I believed I was at fault for this event. After all I had "agreed" to it in the fish shop freezer with Peter as his last blow knocked me to the ground and rendered me unconscious. It was somehow easier to deal with if I had some kind of power over it. But really I had none. Eventually the delusion of responsibility faded and the truth emerged that this was a brutal violation of me that had been planned and executed in a calculated, abusive way. Over years of calculation…not just this event.

Simon instructed their every move. With each one he would get more adventurous in his instruction and the boys complied. The language became foul and deliberately crude – he got them all involved. They taunted me while my body throbbed with pain. My heart was breaking.

Then the weirdest thing happened. We came to the last guy. He was black and gentler than the others. He was probably more hesitant – a little unsure that what they were doing was ok.

He looked deep into my eyes and at the tears rolling down my cheeks and asked softly so that Simon didn't hear, "Are you ok?"

I indicated no with my eyes. I couldn't speak.

The young man got off and said, "Sorry!"

He then played it up to the others to make it look like he was done. He made me feel human again for a brief moment. It was over! My nightmare was done. Aching with pain I watched them all leaving. My heart began to pound again. I could feel blood rushing through my arms and legs again. It was as if I had held my breath the whole time, even though that was impossible as it had been quite some hours. I couldn't wait to get out of there.

I asked if I could use the washroom to "clean up." Simon led me to the bathroom around the corner. The door was opaque glass, but I could see he wasn't moving from the door. I looked for an escape route, but I was still naked. There was a bathroom window but it was at least two stories up and a sheer drop. I went to pee and that's when the real pain hit. Oh my God it burned. I didn't dare look at the toilet paper, but I knew there was blood. I breathed a sigh of relief. It was over. I survived. I could go home and forget about this horrible nightmare.

I went back to the room to get my clothes. They weren't there.

Simon said, "You're not done yet!" He left and I heard the door lock behind him. My heart sank and I broke down in tears. These weren't just rolling tears now, I was full-on bawling my eyes out. I knew I was never going to get out of there. I could hear Simon on the other side of the door on the phone, talking to more men to come down. I was horrified. I couldn't take any more.

Simon came back in and ordered me to stop crying. Then he said one sentence that clarified everything for me; how much he hated women, how he felt about me, and how he had no regard for human life whatsoever…which was dangerous for me. I was really scared. His horrible character, the essence of who he was as a man was summed up in this sentence. That defining phrase was, "There's no difference between fucking your boyfriend's cock fifteen times or fucking fifteen cocks one time. Get over it!" Fifteen? There were going to be ten more? He was going to keep going until I was completely destroyed. I was certain of it. Even after what I had just experienced, those words seemed to tear my heart even more. It repulsed me so much I went back into shock. I couldn't breathe or speak. I halted the crying as the statement sucked the life out of me.

Simon left again for what seemed like an eternity. I was on a terrifying journey that I believed I would never return from. I knew I was as good as dead. Pain was still pulsing through my body like electric shocks. I tried to unlock the door several times even though I knew it was useless. There was another door that led to the balcony. I contemplated running out there naked, but then what? It was now quite late in the evening. By the time anyone paid attention and called the police I believed I would be dead. I was also incredibly humiliated and embarrassed by my experience so far. I ran through an incredible gamut of emotions. Was this how my life was going to end? Was my dead body going to be found washed up on the beach across the street and my photo plastered all over the news? What a terrible punctuation to a life. What had I done to deserve this fate? Would anyone come and save me? I thought not. Hope was now a fantasy.

I didn't try to run anymore. I was fucked by a man with such disregard for humanity that I knew no mercy would be given, and in fact if I had begged for mercy I know it would have made things worse. Suddenly I heard Peter's voice at the door. My hope returned for a moment that I was going to be rescued…however, he had brought beer. Simon had a conversation with him that sounded like, "We haven't finished with her yet." I tried to yell out to him to come and save me. But I couldn't. No voice came out. I tried to move but I had frozen yet again. My body had let me down. My supposed boyfriend betrayed me beyond words.

Simon soon burst in with the next group of men. They were older, drunker, and much more ominous. I lost count of how many there were. I stopped counting at three or four. These men seemed like the underbelly of society; seasoned rapists and all misogynists. Simon was more one of the boys with this group rather than a mob coach. They got right to it. They didn't need any coaxing. It shocked me and I naturally responded with resistance. That was a mistake. All four got on the bed. They held me down and one got on top of my chest and pinned my arms down painfully, not like before where I was just restrained. He hit my cheek hard, which took my awareness away from the pain in the rest of my body. They threw me around like a rag doll. When was this going to end? I'd stopped asking myself how it would end, as I believed I was going to die. I just hoped it would be soon.

I can't remember the chronology for what happened next, but I distinctly remember various moments. I was being poked and prodded from all angles, and not just sex things but cruel things like twisting my nipples until they stayed out. I have inverted nipples and they didn't naturally raise up, so they twisted them until they were swollen and bleeding. I tried to disconnect from my body. I had done it before. But each penetration was like sandpaper, waking me back to reality. I was red raw by this stage, not to mention the fact that no one was wearing condoms, although at this point I couldn't even think about the possible consequences of that. I didn't think I was going to survive it anyway.

One guy had a bent penis that felt like I was being stabbed internally every time he thrust himself inside me. It was excruciating. Obviously that guy couldn't get a date if his life depended on it so this was how he dealt with it. By fucking "some . . . body." That's all I was at that stage; a body, nothing more. I felt completely worthless and powerless. It was like my existence had faded into nothing. Not noticed, deliberately demeaned. The worst feeling in the world. It felt like I was drowning. I had no regard for how I felt. I felt like I was floating under water while debris bumped into me and currents pulled me this way and that. But unlike previous desperate feelings, I wasn't nervous or anxious. I wasn't gasping for air, trying to hold on to anything that went past. I just lay there with arms outstretched like Jesus on the cross, awaiting my imminent death with acceptance.

The pain was intense. The emotional pain even greater. The taunting was the worst. I'd thought the last group had gotten a good handle on humiliating me, but that was child's play in relation to this. All I could taste was the alcohol, while urine and the smell of semen overwhelmed my senses. I was now choking and things went downhill from there. I had had enough. This was way too much for me or anyone to bear. Who could possibly do this? How could anyone be so cruel and so disregarding of another's life? What the hell had happened to these people that made them hate humanity so much?

As I started to choke, I decided this was the time to die. I wanted to be taken. I no longer wanted to survive. I didn't want to face a life of terror knowing this had happened to me. I knew what trauma could do to someone as I had experienced it before, but this was the worst thing I'd ever experienced. Even facing my father's gun wasn't as bad as this. It was literally torture. I didn't care why any more. I asked God to take me, but before I lost consciousness, I felt something break. It felt physical, although it wasn't. I didn't end up with any broken bones. But I snapped. It felt like my soul had ripped out of my body and was never coming back. Less than a second later, I became unconscious. I lost something that day and it hasn't returned since. I have yet to be able to define what it was, but I do feel I left part of my soul in that room. I don't know how to get it back, and until now I haven't really wanted to integrate it back. This is the pull of suicide. This is why it's so appealing. I am only going where the rest of me went that day. I felt like it left me behind. Maybe I will recover it, maybe I won't. But at this stage I don't even want to try. I still want to go back to that moment and die. At least then justice would be served. Those men would be in prison. People would understand the pain I went through. And it wouldn't be that thing you don't talk about.

Sometime later, I regained consciousness. I was across the street, clothed and lying in the gutter. Peter was there. I was vomiting. I could hear the ocean in the distance. It was across the street in the other direction. I really just wanted to walk into the ocean and drown. Peter was behaving like he knew nothing. "What are you talking about? Simon did this? I will kill him!"

My mind skipped a beat and the next thing I remember is being in Peter's house, lying on the floor of the shower fully dressed. The shower was cold. I had vomited up the packet of codeine I had consumed prior to getting in the shower. I didn't even care that I couldn't kill myself. I felt numb. No pain. I didn't even know the shower water was cold except for the fact that I was shivering. I remember nothing more.

On the day I split up with Peter, I had been in dissociation for quite some time but had moved back to my hometown of Sydney. I hadn't finished university yet, but I took a break for a while to work out my life. Something had stirred deep within me around my early twenties. The gang rape had already occurred, but I had not yet extracted myself from the perpetrator. I was actually confused about who the perpetrator was, but once again, deep in my heart I knew. I told Mom that I was going to leave Peter, and she really was relieved. She knew nothing about the rape or abuse, but she knew the type of guy he was. So she said, "How are you going to do it?"

I said, "I don't have to – I will wait until his threat of 'I'm going to leave you if you don't do x, y or z.'"

Sure enough, within a day or two Peter threatened to leave me, and I said, "Ok! Off you go then."

"I mean it!" he said, and he threw a good-sized rock over my parents' house, which could have had a drastic effect if it had hit someone.

"Oh my God, you could have killed someone!" I yelled.

"This is your last warning, once I leave I'm never coming back."

"Well off you go then."

He drove off dramatically (in my car that was in his name due to "insurance" purposes). He waited for me to run after him. I didn't. His plan had failed. He had no power over me any more.

It felt fantastic. I knew there would be a love fest at the end of it. So I waited. A few days went by and no calls, no nothing. A few more days went by and when he realised I was serious, he apologised for his behaviour. I berated him with all my pent- up frustration and anger and told him exactly what I thought of him. He said he would be a better boyfriend. I told him "I told you that you can go and you did. We are done." And I was really done. I never went back. My inner strength had kicked in and nothing was going to drag me back. This voice was strong, but I could only access it in pure anger. It wasn't until much later that I developed this strength at any time I needed, rather than just when I was mad. Even though I was able to access my rage, I certainly didn't deal with it at the time. I still wouldn't have been equipped to deal with it effectively. But I did stand my ground and found my power.

After four years of abuse from Peter, I finally got the courage to find my voice. It was a brief stance and it took me another twenty years or so to find it again, but it was there, shaky yet definitive, and if I found my voice once, I could find it again. The little being that had been born into the world all those years ago was starting to re-emerge.

I E.M.P.O.W.E.R.
HEAL KIT INITIATIVE 4
- OTHERS

~ "For to be free is not merely to cast off one's chains, but to live in a way that respects and enhances the freedom of others." ~ **Nelson Mandela**

OR THE MODERN EQUIVALENT BOOYA! (BECAUSE OF OTHERS you achieve.) Although I don't like this one as much, as it suggests that you only achieve through others and should relinquish your own power, but it is partly true. You really do need others to succeed, especially in healing.

We are not born into isolation. We are not cheetahs, who grow up to be alone. We are a society and we come in groups called families. My definition of "family" is a little different; more *expanded*. Some families are made up of blood relatives and others can be developed over time amongst kindred souls when the blood variety is lacking. Either way we MUST have people in our corner to heal and thrive. We crave connectedness and it's often the lack of this that motivates people to do nasty and not-so-wise things.

I have collected a number of "family" members along the way. Some are blood relatives, but most are not. These are the people who I could call in the middle of the night to say, "I'm in trouble and need your help," and they would show up. The truth is we must have support and when your own family can't provide it adequately, it is our responsibility to seek that support in others. Yes, *our responsibility*, because we need to take charge of our paths and make the healthy choices as discussed in the previous initiative. Part of that is seeking out the things that we need to heal.

When I am feeling really down, I think about how my *others* would view me. Feeling down can be quite isolating and when this occurs for me, I feel disconnected from the world. Whenever I need to fill out a form that has "next of kin" I feel sad, because in this country, I don't have any next of kin. In fact, I could go hiking one day and get lost in the wilderness, and no one would realise I was gone except my work colleagues. It might be days before anyone sent out a search party. This lonely feeling can be devastating sometimes, but then I kick myself out of it by thinking about how my *others* would view my disappearance. Once they found out, I know many people would rally around to help, even those in my own community, whom I live near, or who know me from going to their store or cafe. This is when I can negate the loneliness, as I know it would matter to these people if I disappeared off the face of the earth. This is important in healing, because sometimes you feel like you could disappear. If I thought that it wouldn't make any difference if I was here or not, I might give up hope.

A few years ago I had no one. I couldn't think of one person I could call if I was in trouble. I didn't have any support. At the time it depressed me more and fulfilled my victim thinking. *Nobody loves me.* Well that's no one's fault but mine. I actually isolated myself from society, and then complained about the fact that I was alone. Now I have many people in my corner. I regularly go to the Pure Integrative Pharmacy, and I talk to the holistic advisor there about my health. She has helped me so much, and we're even doing a liver cleanse together. It may not sound like much, but people need to support you in all facets of your life. She supports my health and I have fun chatting with her, and now I have a buddy I can improve my health with by doing a liver cleanse. Another person supporting my wellbeing is my life coach. Giulia is awesome. Neither of these people do the work for me – I do it. I have to seek it out from them, but they help me with expertise in that field. I told Giulia that I want to get my health better, and she helped me set goals and break it down into small steps I can take every day towards my health. She also helped me identify my barriers to achieving my goals. I know it's her job, but I really feel like she is genuinely supporting me. It doesn't stop there. I joined a choir. I like to sing and I have made at least ten friends just through that. They support my singing, and if I said I wanted to perform somewhere they would assist me in making it happen.

I have amazing hiking friends. There's a group of us who all have dogs and we go together regularly on great hikes. The dogs all know each other so they love it and the group often stops for tea or coffee and it's wonderful. I even have business connections all over the world from people with whom I have worked in one capacity or another and share the same integrity. These people stay in my corner. I have people I haven't worked with in ten years that I could call up to help me out with something or who I could put as a reference on my resume.

All that is to say I now have many people in my corner and some with very strong bonds. This has been essential in my healing. You really can't do it alone. You may think you can, but there are always vulnerable moments in life. Why not have a support network of people who can help you in times of need and who are your cheerleaders when you need that extra push to achieve what you want? Once again, you must take responsibility for creating this network. Opportunities will come up all the time but it's up to you to grab them.

Creating this connection is the first step, but then you need to refine the balance between you and others. We have symbiotic relationships with others, and when the symbiosis is out of balance is when things go wrong. If we put others before us at the expense of our own needs, that is out of balance and we suffer. It does not empower and we cannot heal in this way. If we put ourselves above all others and are arrogant; thinking our needs are more important than everyone else's, that equally disempowers us. Our relationships with others need to be truly supportive both ways. At times when we are down, we can rely on the genuine support of others, we can see ourselves through their eyes, and we can ask for help and have them work with us toward our goal of healing, but never take the reins for us. And likewise, we can give of ourselves to assist others in need, not to enable, but to give the support that will be truly healing. I have had some amazing experiences that I have felt were the most supportive moments of my life. You would think it was where someone swooped in and saved the day but it wasn't. No one was there for me when I was being raped. No one was there even after that, as I kept it secret for a long time, but many people have been in my corner helping me heal from this trauma. It was others with genuine intention, who supported me in a moment of healing and they asked for nothing in return.

PHOTO: My hiking group: Cathy, Karen, me, and Fiona. We share a special bond of having experienced a drama, where Zuko, the big Golden boy in the middle, was swept away by the river, and Fiona, the one on the right, and I jumped in to the swollen, freezing river to save him. Sebastien, my dog, is an honorary Golden – lol. Most of the dogs are looking toward the trail.

TRUE SUPPORT

THE PHELANS

Sam was my best friend when I was three years old. Her parents, Marion and Tom Phelan, looked after me during the day from the age of about three until I was about seven. They were awesome. Sam was a tomboy as was I, so we did all kinds of fun stuff like tadpole chasing and Easter egg hunts and tree climbing and bike riding.

In the year 2000, I accidentally ran into Sam at my doctor's office of all places. I was so happy to see her. We hadn't kept in touch, but I never forgot her. She told me that she was working part-time, so that she could do her veterinary studies at university. She will make an awesome vet. She is compassionate and caring, great with animals, and highly intelligent. Sam taught me how to properly pick up a cicada so that it didn't screech. Marion taught me all kinds of cool crafts, and Tom and I had great, intelligent conversations about life when I was the ripe old age of five. I would ask him about the world and he would tell me honestly. They treated me like I mattered; not like a kid with no say. They were my first validation that I was worthy. I remembered their integrity, their kindness and love. It is so important to have some sound foundations of what's right about life from somewhere – even if the people giving you that advice are not related. As a kid, I instinctively knew that they were right – this was how life should be, not the way I lived it with my parents, where things didn't make sense, I was hit for no apparent reason, life was full of violence and fear, and nothing I did or said mattered. I was to be "seen and not heard." – *Silent*.

At the doctor's office, Sam asked if I wanted to go and meet up with her parents as they'd love to see me. Of course I wanted to – I loved them. They were the highlight in my life at a time when Mom and Dad were still together and abuse from my dad was a regular occurrence.

We sat in their all too familiar living room. They'd done some renovations, but the happy feelings I used to get when I visited were still recognisable. Tom Phelan, Sam's dad, talked to me about my childhood. He filled in many gaps that I had. He had been a barrister when I stayed there, but now he was a fully-fledged Queen's Council Judge (QC.) He spoke about my abusive father and told me how we would be brought over to their house when my dad was threatening us with a rifle. I also filled Tom in on my father's other abuse and how violent he was.

Tom was very adamant that I should prosecute my father and said he would support me 100%. He would help me every step of the way. I thought about it seriously, but even in the year 2000 when I saw the Phelans at least thirty years after the abuse from my father, I was still terrified of him. I couldn't even imagine going up against him in court, and I knew that my mother had already tried that many years before to no avail. Even just the suggestion shook me to the core and raised my hyper vigilance substantially. So I kindly said that I wasn't ready to do it at that time, but I would give it serious consideration. Tom left it open for me as an eternal offer without any statute of limitations. I thanked him and told all of the Phelans how nice it was to see them all these years later and how much I'd loved the times I'd spent with them. I had found great people in my corner, and I will never forget Tom's offer even though I know I will never take him up on it.

Maya Angelou said: "I've learned that people will forget what you said, people will forget what you did, but people will never forget how you made them feel."

I never forgot how the Phelans made me feel. It's important in healing to identify these small conversations that mean, "I support you 100%," and not diminish the weight of their sincere meaning. It is big and life altering and when I feel like no one's in my corner I can negate that to say – this family offered help of a substantial kind and I am profoundly grateful. They supported me both in my childhood and adulthood and some days when all seems too much I can think of this family and their support and not feel alone in the world. Someone cared for me and still does, and it's my responsibility to acknowledge it.

SUPPORTERS WHO DON'T EVEN KNOW YOUR NAME - CLARA HUGHES

There are people in your corner who don't even know you exist. Terry Fox fought for cancer awareness for many more generations of people after he died. His efforts supported people long after his death. I felt

Olympian Clara Hughes was doing that for me. I wanted to support her ride across Canada for Bell Canada's "Let's Talk" campaign for mental illness. The funny thing was, I was so depressed I didn't feel like going, but I figured if Clara Hughes could ride 5000kms across Canada through winters and sleet and snow with depression, the least I could do was get my fat, depressed ass out of the house and take five minutes to drive to West Vancouver and cheer her on.

As I sat on the side of the road contemplating the energy and courage of Clara, an eight-time Olympic medal holder (both summer and winter Olympics,) I started to cry. I had connected with someone else's pain and now that I'd connected with it - it opened up my own pain. Thank God most of the people there were touched by mental health issues so they were a little more accepting of my outburst, although I tried to hide it as best I could. Sometimes emotion is like vomit; once it starts coming up, putting your hand over your mouth to stop it is going to have very little effect. I couldn't stop the flow even though I was out in public. Emotion just flowed out of me as I thought about her journey and what she was doing for people like me who also live with mental health issues like depression and anxiety. I don't mind connecting with my pain, but I would prefer to do it in the privacy of my own home, not standing on the side of a road in front of a hundred people waiting for an Olympian to ride past. Anyway, I'd made it there to support her in her support of me and others like me.

Clara suffered depression even while winning Olympic medals. This astounds most people as they think success makes you immune to depression, but it doesn't. It does not discriminate. You could be having a wonderful life, with all the riches in the world, working in your dream job, and you can still be affected by depression. During the 2012 Olympics, Clara interviewed athletes that also suffered depression – she was and still is, shining a light on that which used to be taboo. It's awesome and I have a great deal of respect for her. After all it's not easy to ride across Canada, and it's not easy to tell everybody about your own vulnerabilities.

When I looked around there were only about a hundred people, if that. I thought, here is Clara riding through terrible conditions right across Canada and a hundred people out of 100,000 have turned up to show their support. Admittedly, she was just riding through to the bigger event downtown, but it had been advertised in the paper for weeks. Posters everywhere had flooded the market. . .and one hundred people showed up, mostly people who had a direct relationship with mental illness. Having said that – we made the noise of 100,000 people and we waved our blue support batons and we shouted for the thirty seconds that Clara rode past. I could see on her face how happy and grateful she was for these one hundred people, and that made me cry again. I got the point. Even Terry Fox went through towns where no one knew him or why he was running, but decades after his death, people right across Canada do marathons in his honour and for the legacy he started. He is a household name and he gave a voice to cancer. Even if Clara has few supporters now, the after- effects will be long lasting and it's only because of people like her that mental health will be better known.

At this point she inspires me to keep writing these pages and telling my own story. It's no 5000km bike ride, but it is a marathon. All these words make me process my feelings – they help me and put me on an emotional roller coaster at the same time. They are hard to confront, especially when the stigma of mental health issues like PTSD and depression still hold shame and discomfort in polite circles. I have had Post-Traumatic Stress Disorder (PTSD) for a long time. I was first diagnosed at twenty-one. I am now in my late-forties. I have other diagnoses too, but this is the main one affecting my every day. PTSD doesn't heal on its own. Time does not heal all wounds. PTSD affects all aspects of my life, work, career, relationships, intimacy, finance – everything is affected, but it still seems that because it's not a physical affliction, people don't want to acknowledge it. God bless you Clara, for changing this, one hundred people at a time. Clara is in my corner and because of that I am in hers, although we will probably never meet or speak. There are always people fighting for you if you look hard enough, and it's important to acknowledge that support. You will need it. Seek out others who may have suffered like you. There are many societies and organisations that offer support. It is your responsibility to seek them out if you want to heal.

I E.M.P.O.W.E.R.   103

PHOTO: Clara Hughes ride across Canada for Bell's "Let's Talk" campaign to raise awareness of mental health issues.

GIVING SERVICE TO OTHERS

IT SEEMS EXTRAORDINARILY SIMPLE: "GIVE TO OTHERS," BUT IT'S not. The giving must be of pure intention. There have been many times when I have volunteered my time in a seemingly altruistic manner, however, the balance of others versus myself was not aligned. I would volunteer so that I could feel better about myself, not so I could help others. My intention coloured the action so that it was actually a selfish act. Others too have taken advantage of my giving and manipulated me into me giving them something that was not due or appreciated. The true flow of giving and receiving must be perfectly in balance. It does feel good to truly "give," but if you're expecting something back or only doing it to look good, or fulfilling a need to feel wanted, then it doesn't truly heal. Like all good healing steps, when done correctly, it must take something from you only to give you something twice as valuable in return. I have struggled with this balance. Sometimes I have given to have nothing left for me, at the expense of my own health. That's not healing. And other times I have sought out a balance to my crappy life, and I would try to "use" it to my advantage…also not very healing. Giving must be of pure intention and your heart must be truly open. Then the gifts you receive from it will resonate deeper in your heart than you thought possible.

A MOMENT IN PASSING

"It's too soon!" I said to Mom. Gordon had just passed away on Tuesday and now Sunday was Father's Day in Australia.

That's just cruel. I told Mom they should move it to the Canadian Father's Day, which is earlier in the year, and then she would have a chance to grieve a little. Gordon's death affected me more than I thought. I hadn't even seen him in five years and fortunately I missed the "Parkinson's Dementia years." I wanted to remember him as my stepdad, not a ranting nursing home patient.

He passed away on Tuesday, the 27th of August, 2013, one day after his and my mother's thirty-fifth wedding anniversary. It was one of those moments I knew was coming and was a blessing given his current state, but it doesn't make death any easier on the people left behind to miss him.

For me in Canada, being seventeen hours behind, it was still Monday, the 26th of August, Gordon and Mom's wedding anniversary, and I was about to leave work. Mom's message said, "Pops is fading. With him now." I hopped in the car to go home and thought about my life with Gordon over the last thirty-five years. It was nice memories coming up. I'd cry, and then I'd focus back on my driving to get home safely. The trip home was a journey in itself. It was like I was playing a movie reel of highlights of my life with "Pops." It was nice, but then I got home and waited. Waiting for someone to die to whom you are close and who is in another country, is a very uncomfortable feeling. I tried everything; distracting myself with TV, going with the feeling and trying to let whatever came up be, sending healing, and eating chocolate. Even that didn't work.

It was about four hours later, and I couldn't take it any more. I emailed Mom, hoping not to disturb her too much, but also trying to involve myself in the process. I really wanted to be by his side supporting my mother, but I wasn't. I was 17,000 kilometers away. Fortunately Mom started emailing me back and forth, so I felt like I was with her, but even that distraction faded in efficacy. It was about 9:30 p.m. Monday night, my time, which was 2:30 p.m. Tuesday, Australian time. I really felt like I needed company, but I realised I had no one to call. I could have put a message on Facebook, but it's not enough at a time like this. I actually wanted a live person. This is one time in your life that you need friends or family around to really connect with, but I had no one. This added to my depression.

Totally unable to "do" anything, I just cried. The LAST thing in the world I wanted to do was "give" to anyone in that moment. I wanted to be selfish and feel my grief. Instead I decided to go to sleep sending healing and love to Pops and Mom. I had been unsuccessful earlier at sending healing, but I really committed to it this time. I fought myself really hard so that I could fully engage in the healing. My heart lay totally open and loving.

It was the most incredible healing. This was the most spiritual experience I'd ever had. I started lightly holding my hands over my heart, doing a Buddhist practice called tonglen, where you take negative energy and turn it into positive. As I did this I felt my heart get really warm, and I could feel it beating as if my hands were in my chest. I felt like I was connecting to Gordon's body. It was as if I was lying inside his body. I looked around in it and sent healing to any part that needed it. Then I felt like I was healing the disconnection between his physical and spiritual bodies. I could feel him unpeeling from his physical body and I healed each part as it lifted away. It was so incredible, and the strongest visualisation I've ever had doing healing. At that point I came out of his body and was in a hallway. I was helping Gordon across to the other side, like I was helping my dad get off a train.

He was disoriented at first. He said, "What's going on?"

It was then that an old familiar face came bounding over to greet Gordon as if they were long-lost brothers. It was Uncle Dick, who had died when I was only about ten. He was a lovely man and everybody's favourite uncle. He was actually my stepdad's uncle and I had very fond memories of him. Uncle Dick greeted Gordon with such delight that Gordon forgot to be fearful and was so happy to see him.

Uncle Dick made the perfect life-graduation host. The hallway walls were lined with obvious family members. I say obvious as I was at a funeral once with Gordon's side of the family, and I looked around and everyone looked the same. They had the same unique curly hair, the same bowed leg-shaped bodies, both male and female, and they even stood the same way. It was quite funny. If computer-generated images had been around then, I would have sworn they weren't real people but rather avatars. But they were real, and here they all were again on the "other side." Some hugged Gordon, some shook his hand, and as he walked down the hallway greeting everyone he got happier and happier and physically he became younger and younger. It was as if they had thrown a big surprise party for him. It was awesome. It was the happiest I had ever seen him.

At the end of the hallway were his parents. Gordon paused and turned around. He had not been spiritual at all in life. He was the type to say, "When you're dead, you're dead." He didn't believe in any kind of afterlife or God or spirituality, although over the years he'd come to accept my psychic abilities as I found his wallet many times. Mom would call and ask if I could "see" where it was, and every time they found it where I said, but still Gordon was no convert by any means. As he paused at the end of the hallway he turned and looked at me with a big smile on his face and said, "What is this?" I explained that this was his life-graduation and celebration. It was to be enjoyed and this would be his life from now on. He then asked why I was there. I looked deep into his happy, young eyes and I said, "This is what I do. I am a healer and I help people on both sides." He said a heartfelt thank you and turned around.

I was jolted out of my healing and peace by my iPhone with an email. It was from Mom. It read, "He's gone."

I replied; "I know." August 27th, 2013.

Even though I didn't want to send healing at the time, I opened my heart to it and let it come. My intention was to send pure love to the man I regarded as my father. I wasn't obligated. The rewards were remarkable. This was a time I truly gave to others, and it gave me a totally new perspective. I felt like my life mattered to this person at this time. This was my way to say goodbye to Pops.

PHOTO: Mom and "Pops"

ROARING TWENTIES AND EARLY THIRTIES - SELF DISCOVERY

AFTER LEAVING PETER I PAUSED MY UNIVERSITY STUDIES AND remained in Sydney to recover from the horrific events with him. I moved back in with my mom, and I tried as best as I could to get my life back.

I tried to do things that I loved, all the while keeping secret the events that had transpired. I told no one and tried to lead a "normal" life. I explored who I was in all aspects of my life. Who did I want to hang out with? What did I want to do as a career? What activities inspired me in life?

I BELONG HERE – FINDING MY PEOPLE

SITTING IN MY OFFICE WHERE I WORKED FOR A COLLECTIONS firm in North Sydney in the 1990s and looking out the window from the fifth floor, I saw a huge, dark cloud come across the sky. It was about 4:30 p.m. I had experienced many fabulous, violent storms in Sydney, especially during summer when the days were hot. By the afternoon, a brisk southerly might bring with it a spectacular storm and an incredible light show with thunder and lightning engulfing the sky in a burst of light, too bright to look at. These storms usually leave just as quickly as they come and bring a sense of balance and freshness to the air, but this one was different. The sky is always dark during a storm and you can watch the storm front come across. Where I grew up we had a glass-enclosed dining room overlooking a bay where you could literally watch the storm move in across Middle Harbour in Sydney. You could see the edge of the storm as it whisked through the clanking boats on their moorings. (Finally I got to view the edge of the rain.)

This day when I was in my office, the stormy sky was black as if it was night, though it was a summer afternoon. This was a huge storm; the air changed. You could feel the atmosphere suck in a deep breath before it let go its rage on the city below. We all watched from work knowing that this storm was different. There was a debate whether to stay at work and ride it out or to try to rush home and beat it. The weather made the decision for us. Before we could even decide, loud thunderclaps crashed around the building. We were going nowhere fast. In all my life I had never seen a storm like this one. Winds whipped up papers and debris, even five floors up. It was incredible. I love storms and I am in awe of their power. I was a little happy that I wasn't out in the middle of it. There were fifteen minutes of crashing thunder and spectacular lightning. It even rattled the thick office windows. Then it was gone as fast as it came in. By 4:45pm it had moved on. When I left the building at five p.m. and headed for home I knew that I was going to be called out by the SES (State Emergency Services) where I volunteered. Debris was everywhere; trees down, papers all over, backyard sheds in trees. It was just a mess. Sure enough, as soon as I got home there was a message for me to come in.

We all piled into the truck in our orange jumpsuits. They were actually overalls, but we looked like a bunch of wayward criminals as we arrived at Ground Zero not far from where my office was. I had never seen destruction like it. Streets were completely covered in trees. It was as if a giant had walked through these several North Shore neighbourhoods and lopped off the top halves of all the four-story-high trees. Nothing green was left untouched. Then of course there were the houses. Roofs in neighbours' yards, backyard sheds thirty metres high in the tall trees, clotheslines on their sides. I saw the whole top story of a house upside down in a neighbour's yard. There were many streets that even the big rescue truck couldn't navigate due to downed trees and power lines. The first house we came to we went into the kitchen where there was an elderly lady sitting at the kitchen table still with a cup of tea in front of her, and just behind her was a huge tree through the middle of her house. She was in shock. I sat with her and talked to her trying to find out if she had family we could call, and where she was going to stay. She was a lovely lady. She didn't seem too upset about the house, she was more talking about her cup of tea and that it was getting cold.

In house after house we were navigating around other huge trees in living rooms, bedrooms, or through the whole house. The storm did not discriminate. I was taught at that time how to use a chainsaw. It was great, although I just used the little one to get the branches off the bigger trunks, and then the older guys would come in with their huge chainsaws. One guy lopped off a bit too much and a big slab of trunk fell off and smashed into the only surviving window in the living room. "Oops," he said. "At least it's covered by insurance."

I learned the ropes literally. I saw how to extract a tree from a house without killing everyone around you (very important), and I started taking on more of a counsellor role, seeing as most of the people in SES at that time were male. I tended to the victims and gave them resources to help them to get back on their feet. It was also at this time that I accidentally became the communications officer. No one else wanted to be on the radio, so I took the job. It's pretty hard to maintain radio communication when you're on someone's roof trying to tie down a tarpaulin. So it was left to me. I'd still be on the roof, but wouldn't have to tie anything down. We were there for four days; sleeping and eating in the truck, grabbing water when we could, and going back to the command post for further instructions. It was a great atmosphere of community. Nothing made me feel more connected to the world than being able to help people in need and truly make a difference. I helped find people's precious belongings in what was left of their houses. I calmed people down and worked with them to find solutions for whatever they needed, all while communicating important information back to the incident command post, such as injuries, equipment required, and anything else emergency-related. Because of the huge area affected there were many

I E.M.P.O.W.E.R.

volunteers, and radio access was quite limited. So I had to learn on my feet and figure out what to prioritise, but I found I was really good at it.

I call these moments "the time of my life." I shone, I loved it, I lived and breathed it. Not because of the devastation obviously, but because I felt I had a purpose, and I was good at it. I remained calm, was exceptional at making quick decisions in times of stress, and I loved counselling people. I had a knack for it. *It would be great if I could do this for a living*, I thought. *I feel like I was designed for this type of work. Doing this, I know why I am here.*

It did bring me back to reality when I went back to work and saw my pay slip greatly diminished. Fortunately, the government had laws preventing the company from firing me, but it didn't mean they made it easy for me; they made snide remarks and I felt my dismissal was imminent. Despite that, I had indeed found my people in the emergency field; I just didn't know how to integrate that with paying my bills.

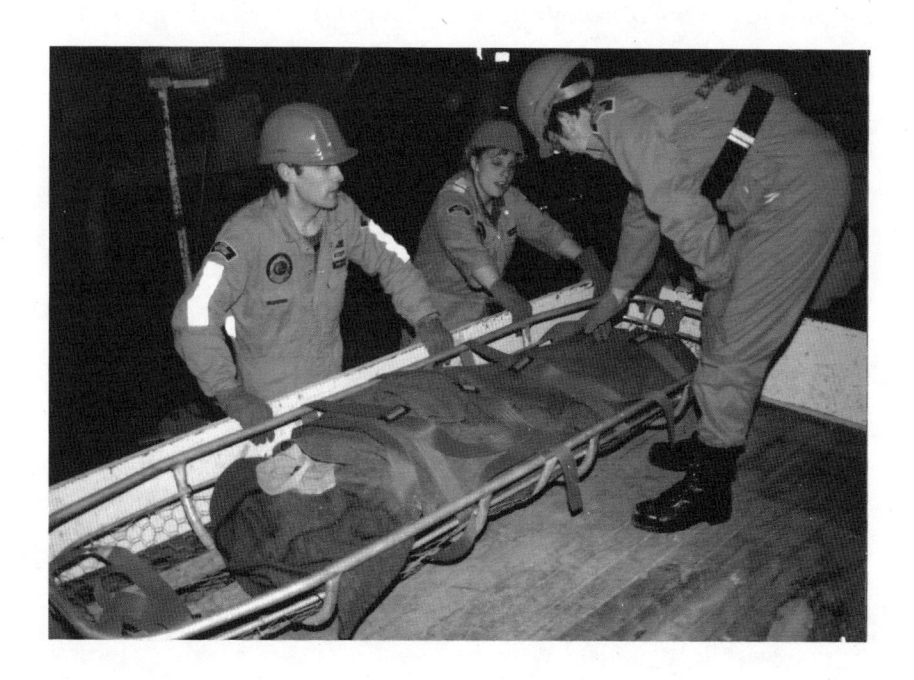

State Emergency Services New South Wales circa 1990 at a training exercise.

Another thing I did during this period was to volunteer my time back at my old school to help them with their theatre production. I still loved theatre and wanted to be around it. It was there that I met Stephen, an art teacher at the school and my husband to be. He was a breath of fresh air after Peter and had no abusive tendencies at all. Still, being co-dependent at the time, I craved his love and attention. When we first got together I spent the whole weekend with him, and when we were apart I didn't function as a whole person. Although unhealthy, it was still a step up from Peter.

Stephen and I moved in together and we married rather quickly amongst rumours of a baby, although no such baby existed. It was just two dysfunctional souls recognising each other and connecting deeply to enable the dysfunctions. I don't regret that as it did provide me with some recovery from a very disturbing and challenging relationship. I could lean on someone. Of course it wasn't going to last; dysfunctional relationships never do unless the dysfunction remains.

I had tried to hold down a regular job, however, that proved difficult. Keeping such a big secret affected everything I did. I ended up cleaning houses and making do with what I could. The relationship with Stephen was safe and comforting but the events that had occurred started to fray the edges.

Three years later, the draw of finishing my university degree was too loud to ignore. I convinced Stephen to move with me back to North Queensland to complete my final year. He did so begrudgingly and ended up with a fantastic job at the aquarium where he designed and built the exhibits. I finished university and went off to start my career in theatre directing. It was at this point as I gained my strength for who I was that I realised as "safe" as Stephen was, he didn't provide much else. I was growing up and safety is great but it's not love. As my expression of myself grew and I succeeded in directing plays across Queensland, my need for "safety" diminished and Stephen and I parted ways. He never knew the truth about what had happened to me. He didn't even believe that domestic abuse occurred, so how could someone so naïve take on what I had hidden? We parted ways. I continued with my theatre activities and became a little nomadic while I moved around the country directing plays and teaching theatre.

THEATRE YEARS

LIFE IS OFTEN ABOUT FINDING THOSE THINGS THAT FULFIL YOU from the inside out. For me, directing theatre was one of those things. I had many amazing experiences while directing. When all the pieces came together it didn't just make a picture, it was a six- sense assault that for those who witnessed it took as much away from it as all the collective energy that put it together plus all the audience members. I was an exceptional theatre director and was able to pull the best out of people even beyond what they thought themselves capable of. It used all of my skills, both creative and business, and I absolutely loved it.

One time in a scene from *Camelot*, I had created a battlefield, and I had a stirring bagpiper play and walk through the aftermath of the battle with fog machines and eerie lighting. I was busy running the lighting desk and paying attention to my cues, when the power of the scene itself hit me. It was a resonant moment where I knew that I had created something special, that others were feeling too. There was something that connected with humanity and made people recognise their own hearts. But it wasn't just me. The musicians, the singers, the actors, the fog machine guy, the lighting technicians – everyone had collectively focussed their energy, and it was captured in a moment where all who witnessed it could feel something special. These are the moments we live for. These were the moments that kept me living.

At the end of the show I had a line-up of people wanting to tell me what a great show it was and most of them specifically mentioned that scene. Even some of the cast members had realised something spiritual had occurred, and they too commended my creation of pulling all the parts together. This is one of the things in life I am very good at. I can pull things together creatively and put them in a way that others can relate to. I am hoping this book does just that, but this is a new discipline for me. I knew my place in theatre and was familiar with its inner workings and how to get the best out of people.

These truly are the magic moments of life that extend beyond the physical realm to connect people with their hearts. I hope I find this again as I know I won't be doing any theatre directing any time soon. But it is my expression of me. And as turbulent as my teens and early childhood had been I was certainly blessed for these later moments where I discovered myself. I feel like my twenties and thirties were held together by these resonant moments. They got a little lost in my forties as I spring- cleaned the cupboard to remove all the junk and heal my past misfortunes, and hopefully my fifties will be the pure, clean me, and the resonant moments will return.

FINDING LOVE - DAVID - BEST LOVE EVER

WE FIRST MET AT CAIRNS LITTLE THEATRE SCRIPT WORKSHOP, which I was facilitating. I was pleasantly surprised by the level of competency at this little community workshop. We analysed plays, words, scenes, and subtext and my excitement grew. I always loved fellow thespians (yes, I said thespian), who were at the same level as me in relation to understanding texts. My energy would bounce off people like that, and then it made me a better workshop facilitator. Everyone got more out of the day in those cases.

We analysed, we probed, we explored, and theorised all there was to establish from the scripts we were working with. We left no innuendo unturned, no character unclear, no intention undiscovered. One particular man caught my enthusiasm. He had it going on. This was David. Who was this man asking me very in-depth and profound questions? We debated this way and that, at some points taking over the workshop until I caught myself and got back on track. I was enthralled. Of course he stayed back after class to talk to the "teacher," although I was more a student of his than the other way around.

David and I were inseparable from that point on. I still had a few months left of directing theatre productions in his area, so we got together a lot. David was a fulltime writer and was also a radio host. I got to go on his radio show and promote the theatre productions I was working on, and our energy bounced off each other. We were in the zone. He was a true soul mate. He would tell me how brilliant I was and I would dismiss it immediately. We enjoyed our great debates, and for the first time I actually loved the fact that I could just be myself and he loved me anyway. We loved our simple pleasures of a nice meal or watching the sunset in Northern Queensland where he lived. We were on the same page with everything.

Then came time to leave the area. I had a new city to teach theatre directing in and I had to go about 1500kms away. David had become so much a part of my life I didn't notice that we had fallen in love with each other. Love was the last thing on my mind as I had recently split up with Stephen, my husband of four years, and also David was twenty-five years my senior. Which these days probably doesn't sound like much, but I was only in my twenties at the time. It didn't hit me until I'd packed my car up and was ready to drive off. Just as I was about to leave he said, "You always have a room in my house that's yours whenever you want it." I didn't quite know what that meant until later. As I drove off there appeared a huge hole in my life where David used to be. I missed him terribly.

Soon it became apparent that despite the distance we were meant to be together. Three-hour phone conversations were common. David told me that he had been in love with me the whole time. I had been oblivious until he wasn't there anymore. We really chatted; we got to know each other at a deep level, even more than when we were together. Three to four hours would go by in a heartbeat. Eventually we couldn't stand it anymore and David hopped in a car and drove the 1500kms to be with me between his writing projects. He stayed a few weeks and we grew incredibly close during that time. He was so respectful and loving I almost couldn't handle it, and then it happened – he asked me to marry him. I was shocked, although I needn't have been. I hadn't even told my family about him due to the fact that he was much older than me, and I didn't want to have to deal with the disapproval from them. I was very nervous about marrying someone that was old enough to be my father. Was I just playing out my dysfunctional father relationship? I'm sure any counsellor would have thought so. Or was my reluctance more of me trying to run away from intimacy? I was very good at analysing and theorising, but when it came down to what was really going on, I was lost. I often got confused as to which was the right way and which was the wrong way to go. It's like my radar was broken because I had gotten it so wrong in the past. I no longer trusted myself, let alone someone else.

I'm sure that having a bi-polar father where good was bad, and right was wrong also had something to do with my broken radar. It actually took me a long time to untangle those webs. I eventually figured it out by listening to my heart as we have an inner sense of right and wrong even as children. My difficulty and confusion, though, came from the fact that my heart and soul had become so badly disfigured during the gang rape I didn't even know how to listen to them anymore.

David noticed my hesitation. He said he would marry me but under one condition. He knew something traumatic had happened to me. I'd never spoken about it but he knew me too well, and he knew that it was sexually related. I obviously couldn't hide the fact that I would burst into tears for no apparent reason when we were intimate. Sometimes I could shut it off but not very often. I either burst into tears or shut down physically and emotionally. I knew that David knew I had been raped, but I wasn't ready to face it myself yet. I hadn't spoken about the gang rape to anyone, and I wasn't about to. David reassured me he would help me every step of the way; he would come to counselling with me, he would do anything to support me, but he knew that to be real, we had to go there. I couldn't even admit it to myself. I had memories about it like it was nothing. It didn't matter…it didn't affect me. Technically I "agreed" to it so I couldn't call it rape. I didn't like it but it was fine. That's what I had told myself. I was totally in denial because it was safe. So if I was with a man who reflected back reality – I was no longer safe. I would have to confront my horrific trauma, and I simply wasn't mature enough to do that at that time.

Consequently, I ran as fast as I could in the opposite direction. I wasn't ready to talk about it – not even with my counsellor, so there was no way I could face it head on and with someone I loved! The thought of talking about it or even thinking about it terrified me. So I did the natural thing; I hooked up with another abusive man instead. This was what I was familiar with. I was comfortable there. I didn't have to be real and I knew how the relationship went. A happy, healthy relationship was totally foreign to me, and I really didn't know how to behave in one. I couldn't allow real love in – that would mean I'd have to confront the gang rape. I wouldn't have survived. The negative energy from it was so powerful I would have taken my own life for sure, even with David's support, and in fact, especially with his support. How could I open my heart to trust a man I loved again? Both Dad and Peter had made that next to impossible, or at least I would have to significantly heal to achieve it.

Even with all that and with me running off with some other guy, David was calm and respectful. He knew exactly what I was doing and why, (which pissed me off even more), and he told me exactly what was going to happen. He said, "You will be with him until the abuse gets worse and it becomes too much. You will eventually realise what you've done and you will contact me to tell me you're sorry and you're coming back to me. And you know what? I will be waiting. I will be there to catch you when you fall."

What? He'll be waiting? Is he crazy? He must be . . . I thought to myself, which was even more justification for me to leave. Of course the new boyfriend forbade me to see David and I dutifully complied as I always did. . . just to the wrong person.

Well it doesn't take a genius to figure out that David was right. About a year later there I was, calling him and apologising profusely for being such an idiot. The boyfriend turned abusive and I had trouble shaking him as his brother was a policeman and he kept tracking down my address. Finally, I moved around enough for him to lose track, but it was scary. So even though I realised what a gift I'd had with David I still wasn't ready to deal with my shady past. I asked him if he'd moved on.

He said, "Of course not, I'm in love with you."

Although he was very forgiving I felt really bad. I couldn't face my reality yet, but that left me in some weird limbo. I told David how I was feeling, and he understood. We still chatted for hours. At the end of the conversation I told him we wouldn't be able to keep chatting like this as it killed me to be away from him. But I also I knew I wasn't ready to delve into my shadows yet either. I was caught between a rock and a hard place. David pleaded with me and told me he would help me work through the rape. It was like the psychiatrist I saw in my teens, begging me to let him help me work through my trauma, and once again I rejected it, not yet knowing how to safely deal with my issues without being suicidal. So even though it appeared I was moving away from healing, I was protecting myself and rightly so as I really didn't have the skills to deal with things outside of a therapist's office.

David said we didn't even have to have sex until I was ready, but I couldn't. Every breath I spent with him drew me closer and would eventually force me to face my fears. I knew I wasn't ready but I did promise him this. "I know I will face these things one day and as soon as I do, you will be the first person I call. I promise you that." We parted again. It broke my heart . . . again. That was 1997.

I E.M.P.O.W.E.R.
HEAL KIT INITIATIVE 5
- WISDOM

~ "The doorstep to the temple of wisdom is a knowledge of our own ignorance." ~ **Benjamin Franklin**

BEING WISE USUALLY MEANS YOU HAVE EXPERIENCED SOMEthing and learnt from it. In practicing TIEWIN you absolutely need feedback that you are on the right path, or you won't continue with it. There has to be a payoff. You can't just say, "This is exactly what I need," and your whole life falls over and DOESN'T get better. That would just be nuts. There have always been signs that I was either on the right path or not on the right path, and wisdom must be gained or something isn't working. Signs are always there, they may be in the deepest part of our souls, but they are there. Even when I was a little kid being abused by my father I knew inherently that something was off, I shouldn't be suffering abuse from my main carer. Like a seed, it had all the genetic makeup it needed to come to fruition, but without light and water, without an opportunity to be given room to grow, it lay dormant, just like my empowerment. As a teenager I didn't know any different, no one showed me the light, so I didn't recognise I was in darkness, and I never sought out the light until I knew it existed. But the signs of wisdom were always there. Had I read this book early on in my relationship with Peter I may have been able to empower myself, because it would show me the way. The wisdom is there within; you don't need to look outside for it. We are all empowered beings, it's just that some of us choose not to make the decisions necessary to fulfil that seed's growth.

INSANITY – DOING THE SAME THING AND EXPECTING DIFFERENT RESULTS

ONE OF THE MOST OBVIOUS SIGNS THAT YOU ARE NOT MOVING forward is in Albert Einstein's definition of insanity: "Doing the same thing over and over and expecting different results." From very young I wanted to be a police officer. Growing up they didn't have female officers, then there was a height restriction, then when they relinquished that and I applied I was denied due to my asthma, then I tried again in my forties and once again, something I had no control over prevented my progress. After years of trying I needed to accept that perhaps this wasn't the career for me. If I had gone on *American Idol* each year and kept getting rejected and they said how terrible I was, I would have to have learned from the wisdom of that, and if I kept trying then I would certainly be proving Einstein's theory of insanity. However, that's the obvious wisdom – you don't need Yoda to tell you that. The other side of that coin is that just because something hurts doesn't mean it's the wrong path. More often than not – it means you are doing well.

WISDOM IN THE PAIN

I MAY HAVE BEEN IN PAIN AFTER I QUIT MY JOB AT THE ADULT training centre. Money was more than tight; I had cornflakes for Christmas dinner while I gave my dog the steak as I had run out of dog food, but it was a different type of stress and unhappiness. I knew wholeheartedly that there was wisdom in my decision and I felt better all throughout my body, mind, and spirit. The anniversary of my marriage split fell on Family Day in BC Canada. I could do nothing but feel the pain.

My heart was literally so sore on Family Day, February 10th, 2014, I wouldn't have been surprised if I was actually having a heart attack. I'd had shooting pains go up my neck and into my head, and my heart area just felt heavy and sore. I missed the nice moments with Angie, but having said that, I was fully aware that it wasn't going to work. Imagine how your heart feels when it IS the right person with the right connection, if this is how you react when it is not right. My heart was heavy and there was nothing to do but feel. After I allowed this sadness to wash over me, it disappeared. I was incredibly sad, though that meant that I was positively on the right path and I knew it. It's a different feeling. If you find yourself continually depressed, (from a specific stimulus – I am not referring to the type of depression that just shows up and doesn't want to leave), then maybe there's something you are not paying attention to. The depression is just there to help you figure it out. Entrenched within whatever you are feeling lies a great wisdom if you know what to look for.

The clearest sign for yourself to indicate how well you are healing is not how you are feeling, but rather how you feel about yourself. If you find that you are constantly berating yourself, that you are angry and feeling negative and nothing in your life is going well, you can be fairly certain that you have more work to do. Alternatively, if you are moving through your pain, if some goals you want to achieve are suddenly getting closer, then you can be reasonably sure that whatever you are doing is good for you.

WHAT ARE YOU SENSITIVE TO?

The next issue is: How do you know what to work on? Well that part is easy. You follow what you are sensitive to. You don't need to be in a mindful state to notice that the girl at work who arrogantly thinks she owns the place when she really doesn't have a clue, gets your goat every time and turns you into an angry mess. It's reasonably obvious that if this is the case, you haven't yet healed that part of yourself that has been affected by arrogant people, or maybe it's a reflection of your own arrogance at times.

Less obvious is whether or not you are living authentically. If this arrogant, clueless person at work happened to be your boss, that would indeed affect your daily work life. If it's a co-worker, you can possibly do things to work through your own stuff so that the person doesn't affect you as much, but when that person is someone making career decisions for you and is a reflection of the company you work for, you may not be living authentically if you stay in that job. The wisdom in that is, "What type of company allows people like that into high positions who can affect your career so negatively?" Is that really a company you want to work for? And if you are sensitive walking into work every day and your patience is thin, you can be sure something about it is inauthentic for you.

I was confronted with that very decision myself at the training centre. My boss was brilliant and certainly got the job done but at great consequence to all who dealt with her. I had many colleagues in tears over her treatment of them, not to mention my own struggles. It's at that point I saw the wisdom in the situation and realized that it wasn't going to change, so I moved on. Had I stayed it would have caused me great unrest and I wouldn't have been able to heal. I paid attention to how sensitive I was to my boss and how I felt after any interaction with her. That was my key catalyst for making the decision to get out. The fire event was just the trigger, but the sensitivity was how I felt after her call at the fire and how I felt walking into work every day after that – that was my moment of wisdom.

WISE MISTAKES

Now just before you go and berate yourself for not having stood up and empowered yourself until now, let me just point out some more wisdom. Some of the greatest achievements have been made from the biggest mistakes. There is undeniably wisdom in the mistakes we make. I am a prime example of a huge mistake or misstep that my very existence depends on. My mother was in a horribly abusive relationship with my father. Let's say she did stand up for herself very early in the piece and empowered herself so that she didn't suffer years and years of abuse. If she had done that I wouldn't have existed at all. I was the last child out and I occurred long after the abuse started. So don't go wiping out your past too quickly. The mistakes and missteps where you are still trying to figure things out can be just as powerful and necessary as the times you take right action and step up for yourself. I am living proof. Had my mother figured out how to leave my father earlier I wouldn't be here writing this book. I wouldn't have even made it to the planet. Imagine that! Thank you Mom, for the biggest mistake you ever made. I am literally eternally grateful.

NOTICING MEANING

NOTICING MEANING. "WHY ME?" IS OFTEN THEN QUESTION that is asked when a trauma occurs. It sounds pathetic but the reality is, it comes for all; it's just that some people move through it faster than others. Ultimately it is our way of making sense of the event.

"What did I do to deserve this?"

"What could I have done to prevent this?"

All normal questions when your life is going along happily, and then, usually in a space of seconds, everything changes. Nothing will be the same again. You were talking to someone one minute and the next they dropped dead on the floor. You were chatting on the phone to a friend who was in the car, and then the line went dead. You kissed your son goodbye in the morning and sent him off to school and moments later he's lying in the middle of the road in front of the school bus. We always want to know why. It's human nature, but it is the wrong question. We ask "why" because we want to understand how this occurred; like it would bring some kind of peace if we could make sense of it. But how can you make sense of something that doesn't make sense?

Why did my Auntie Mandi have to die of a brain tumour and not the grumpy old man next door? Why did Mom have to get an autoimmune disease that crippled her from age thirty-four, when she was an aspiring athlete? Why are people cut down in the prime of their lives by an ailment like Parkinson's, dementia, or Alzheimer's? They just got their "wise badges," and now they don't get to use them. What a waste, spending a lifetime gathering wisdom, and then your brain goes to mush so you can never enjoy it! That's just cruel and it happens all the time. Where's the meaning in that? How many times have you heard that people have died straight after they retire?

How can we make sense of it then if "why?" isn't the question? *"Ask not for what your country can do for you but what you can do for your country." - JFK.* I suggest a similar approach for how you can notice meaning during times of crisis. Instead of asking "Why did this happen to me?" rather ask, now that it has happened, "What can I do with this experience?"

I found something more devastating than, "Why did the gang rape happen to me?" I found that if I believed that I had something to do with it like it was my fault somehow; if I knew in advance that it was going to happen, I should have left Peter, I should have done many things other than what I did leading up to that moment, then that at least gave me some power over it. If I had something to do with it, it gave me some kind of control. But when I realised that it had absolutely nothing to do with me; that it honestly could have been anyone with opportunity and submissiveness, that the answer to that question was that I was there and available - it devastated me.

The answer to the "Why?" question was, "Why not? Shit happens!" I could not make sense of that, I could not claim any responsibility or control, so I just had to accept the devastating reality that there was no real rhyme or reason; it just was due to the people involved and their own selfish journeys! It's then that I had to expand my thinking outside of the "Why?" question to something else before I drove myself crazy. I expanded it to ask, "What can I do with this to help others? What if I adopt TIEWIN here?" I am not saying that gang rape is exactly what I needed, but once it happened, if I treated it that way, then the only question left would be, "Why is it exactly what I need?" What good can come of this? How can I use this experience to help myself heal and help others do the same? Trauma will happen, the important question isn't "Why?" it's "What are you going to do about it?"

The second part to the "what" not "why" theory is that in your life after trauma your feelings will be triggered by situations that somehow reflect your trauma. Anytime I see injustice where selfish people do something that positively impacts them, and negatively impacts others, I flip out. Now, I don't need to figure out where in my past that feeling stems from. Old-school psychology would identify, why you're feeling this or that.

Who cares? I don't need a degree in psychology to know where it comes from. However, I do need to acknowledge and feel the feeling: What am I feeling? Obviously I have had some pain in relation to injustice and I need to release some of it. The way I release it, is by taking right action long-term. In the immediate instance I can use mindfulness to help express the feeling, and I can use expansion by way of TIEWIN, and that puts me in the right place to be able to take right action and empower myself. I still may cry and have a deep emotional reaction, but that's all I need to do. I find that what I'm feeling reveals itself in its absolute form. I don't need to trace it back to its origin to heal it. I just need to feel it. Over time the reactivity lessens as long as you take action toward healing it. Ignore it and it will fester. Understand the wisdom of the trigger. Identify what you are feeling, because more often than not – there is no wisdom in the why. Accidents happen, people are in the wrong place at the wrong time, people make bad decisions about who they hang out with or who they marry. "Why?" can lead to a merry-go-round of endless, unanswered questions and focus on the past. "What am I feeling?" focuses on the present moment.

There is one more reactivity I need to discuss. All of this has been about sensory triggers, but additionally there are emotional pattern triggers. For example, if your life used to be under threat by someone who had a pattern of giving you gifts after they abused you, then other intimate relationships may be coloured by that, and the pattern of them giving you a gift may put you into a tailspin as you "know" what will follow. This too is like the stimulus and response. Figure out *what* set you off and identify that it's the pattern of what happened that triggered you, not the person in your life now. I have a general rule of thumb to live by: It's simply breathe through your reaction to yourself before taking any action, and if you feel that your reaction is way out of proportion to the stimulus, then obviously it's your past not your present that you need to deal with. Emotion can overwhelm at any time, especially for those with

PTSD. That's ok, it's not the emotional reaction which is damaging, it's what we do with that reaction. There is wisdom in your own patterns. Investigate them but most importantly feel whatever you are feeling.

So twenty-three years later was the next time I felt that extreme worthlessness in my life. I felt like I had a crappy job with crappy relations, and I was unhappy and depressed; I felt like nothing in my life had meaning. I was stuck asking the same question: Why am I in a crappy job where people prove my sense of worthlessness when I have so much more to offer? Why am I in a relationship where my wife treats me like I don't matter? Why does my family abandon me every time I need them?

When I left my wife my sister called me and yelled at me for leaving such a lovely person. "How could you?"

She had never even met my wife and knew nothing about the relationship and whether or not it was healthy. So why did I believe her words to me that I was worthless? Why did I stay in a job where the people had no respect for who I am or what I can do? When I stopped to notice the meaning in all these events and assumed that they were trying to tell me something, I could then start to ask the question, "What am I going to do about it?" I realised that my present circumstances were telling me that I was stuck in my past-life patterns.

So I left the marriage, and I stopped asking for help from my family as I knew they were incapable of giving it. I got out of the crappy job, and although it took me a while to find the right one, I didn't stop trying. As soon as I stopped asking, "Why me?" and instead asked, "What am I going to do now?" I took back my power. I still assessed what I could have done differently in those situations to prevent them from happening, and in every case it was that I hadn't stood up for myself and taken right action when I could have. My responsibility to my healing now is to make sure I make the right choices and take the hard road that is supportive of my healing. That way I will prevent more of these problems from occurring. The meaning is still important; it yields wisdom. When we are wise we make better decisions for our lives.

Noticing meaning is not asking, "What is the meaning behind what happened to me?" but rather asking, "What meaning can I give this in my life now that it has happened?" Often people get stuck on replaying the moment of trauma over and over hoping to somehow change the outcome.

"If only I'd done CPR on the hard floor and not the bed he might have survived."

"If only I hadn't argued with her she wouldn't have driven off like that and would have seen the train coming."

"If only I hadn't gone out with Peter after the 'please take me back' phone call."

Over and over. No matter how many times you replay it, the reality is that it won't change anything. But maybe I can give his life meaning by teaching CPR in schools. Maybe I can give her life meaning by learning how to argue respectfully and making sure I never use those angry words again as they may be the last words I give a person. Maybe I can write a book to share my healing journey, so that others can benefit from my healing. These options are healing. Berating yourself for not knowing that CPR has to be done on a hard surface, is keeping you stuck in pain and doesn't honour the passing of the person. "If onlys" can be endless. You can "if only" anything. "If only I had known how to do CPR" may as well be, "If only I hadn't had a child." It's just as valid. "If only" is disempowering and does not embrace reality. Look for the wisdom instead. It has happened. "What next?"

THE WISDOM OF RAGE

Rage can be great! As I've said, it's an inevitable bi-product of trauma. Often our reaction to it is to recoil and avoid it at all costs. It definitely has its time and place but when you can, feel it in a healthy way. At the bottom of the barrel is the good stuff. What you really lost is clarified for you. Waiting at the dregs of your rage is a clarity you don't normally have access to, and rage doesn't often rear its head either. So you need to grab the window of opportunity as it arises, if it's possible, while being able to stay safe.

In my early twenties, before I'd even known that something was wrong, I was driving down a large hill towards an intersection, and on the cross street I saw Peter walking back to his car from the bank. It was a busy street and Peter was parked on the side of the road. I had just turned the corner when I noticed him on the roadside of the car about to open his door – well actually, it was my door. I had paid for the car years before, but he had convinced me it was better for insurance purposes to put it in his name. At the very sight of the man who'd caused me so much pain, I was suddenly possessed with rage. It surged through my body until I felt I was going to pop. It was an actual physical sensation. Before I knew what I was doing my foot slammed on the accelerator and I gunned it straight for Peter with every intention of slamming into him, and then the car "formerly known as" mine and ramming it with such force it would go right through the bank.

I had never felt rage like this. I had felt anger, but more suppressed and muted. Given the right circumstances I believe everyone can "go postal," at some point, and this was my breaking point. I had snapped, beyond control, slipping into temporary insanity as I felt the pressure increase on the gas pedal, my knuckles now white, gripping the steering wheel just to make sure I didn't miss the target. I held this state for a good few seconds and they seemed to be the longest seconds of my life. But then I breathed an extraordinary exhale; almost like a last breath. Something caught my eye and snapped me out of my psychotic trance as I sped through the intersection. It was my sanity returning. It made me pause just enough to change the direction I was heading and I went towards home instead, now breathing heavily. Almost hyperventilating, my breaths seemed to draw in down to my toes and were forced out like I was at the doctor's office getting my lung capacity checked. It took all of my will and strength to drive away against the better judgement of my pure anger.

I don't remember anything after that, but I know the experience rocked me to the core. I was scared of what had almost happened, of what I was capable of. Could I really be just like them? This thought saddened me a lot. Had I just turned into the very thing I loathed, which caused me so much pain and suffering? Could I understand them better from this perspective? Having uncontrollable rage? The answer was no. Aversive rage is not healing. It's not insightful. It's destructive and I knew if I didn't do something about it – it would destroy me. The experience scared me so badly I decided to go get counselling.

My rage at Peter was my first clue that something was deeply wrong. Until then I had been in a fog of denial. I was "fine." Well, the fact that I felt like ramming my car into someone was an obvious sign that I wasn't fine, however, it was the rage that triggered that response. It bubbled up like an unstoppable force, expectorating from my being. The good thing is that within my rage, after I had controlled the action and NOT slammed into my ex-boyfriend, I was able to begin my healing journey. Finally, I realized just how much the gang rape had affected my soul, and off I went to a psychiatrist to help me sort out what was what. This was the wisdom of my rage.

Now it may seem like it should have been smooth sailing from that point on, but it took me fifteen years to tell my whole story to the psychiatrist. We picked at it piece by piece and eventually uncovered the soul of the rage and the wisdom of my pain. Just acknowledging it brought about healing. Without that initial rage I could have trotted along in denial for perhaps the rest of my life. My every decision would have been coloured by it, and I would be none the wiser, wondering why my life was so messed up. Rage is the engine light coming on to tell you to take your car to the shop and get it looked at. What is the light telling you? Go to the professionals to get some help in sorting it out. They have the manual, and they can more easily check you over to say, "That's your oil light," and give you the right advice to fix the issue.

I had to have the right support around me to figure it all out, otherwise I could have been overcome by it. Still, somewhere deep inside me had been the foresight to get help when I needed it. I could never have healed without diving into this abyss, and I could never have survived the abyss without professional help as well as support from whom I saw as "family" at the time. Rage is wise, but because it's such an overwhelming emotion – it's a good idea to take it to the shop and let the professionals help you.

WHAT GIFTS HAS MY TRAUMA BROUGHT?

~ "You gain strength, courage, and confidence by every experience in which you really stop to look fear in the face. You are able to say to yourself, 'I lived through this horror. I can take the next thing that comes along.'" ~ **Eleanor Roosevelt**

FURTHER THAN THAT, YOU CAN INVESTIGATE YOUR TRAUMA (AT a later date once you've grieved all the losses and been mindful of all the negative emotions that need to come up), and then you can start to be open to seeing what positive things have come out of the trauma. For me one thing is how strong I really am. I must have so much resilience to have come this far in life and still be ok. I used that deep inner spirit that I was born with, to survive and thrive through all of these experiences. They have helped me bring about who I really am. I haven't come out unscathed, but that's not what life is. Life is the richness, the scars, the crevices, the twists, and the turns. That's what life REALLY is. And the way I have come though to the other side is a testament to my incredible strength. I didn't get the easy road to success, and I'm not sure if anyone does. True power and success is getting up after you are knocked down, and life may look different when you walk ahead, but you are still moving. Those who "die" emotionally at the time of trauma are those who need more healing. Trauma is your opportunity to bare your scars to the world and say I'm still here! The inner spirit I arose from is evident now. Life has given me this opportunity to experience it at a deeper level. My trauma PROVES my extreme resilience. It's not just a theory that should I be in that circumstance I believe I would be ok. It did happen and I am ok. It would be nice if others acknowledged that gift, but first I need to acknowledge it, then others will see it too.

Thirty and Forty-Something - Wheels Falling Off

AFTER DAVID AND THEN LEAVING ABUSIVE GUY NUMBER-TWO, to recuperate I moved back in with my mom and gave up the tiring and not very well-paid jobs I was getting as a theatre director. As much as I loved them I couldn't sustain a good living, and I needed somewhere to call home after travelling to different cities to direct plays. Mom and Pops had since moved from Sydney to the Gold Coast in Southern Queensland. In 1998 I found a good "fill in" job that paid the bills at a Call Centre until I figured out what was my burning desire to do for a living. Little did I know this would be the job that tided me over for the next ten years and also afforded me the opportunity to move to Canada. The unplanned events are often the ones that make a bigger impact and take you to places you never thought possible. If I'd stayed in theatre I probably wouldn't have had the chance to move to North America. What I had deemed to be a "fill in," turned out to be my main career.

A few years later I was promoted to manager and had moved back to my hometown of Sydney. As much as I loved Queensland, it was hot and small. Sydney always drew me back. My depression and general sense of well-being were ok, but I could feel the murmur like a deep rumble of unsettled waste, gurgling to the surface. I felt like I had dealt with a lot of baggage and yet the one event remained untouched. I realised I could never heal fully without addressing this issue. While my business career took off, my personal life started to fray. This was a good sign. If I'd let it fester any longer it would have destroyed many things in my life; it would always force my decisions, and cause general unrest in any relationships.

Early in 2002, when reviewing my life circumstances as I usually did at the end of one year and the beginning of another, I changed my course of direction. I dropped things that weren't working and nurtured things that were. I brought back things I still thought about, maybe giving them a second chance. I had to do something drastic to heal. I returned to counselling and started heading toward talking about the sexual assaults.

More than ten years had passed, and yet I couldn't talk about it, though I was well on the way. I was talking about the nightmares I was having. I couldn't quite put the pieces together, but I was being more real with myself. It was quite debilitating dealing with major traumas one day and going to work and being "normal" the next. It was so tiring that sometimes I was so depressed and exhausted, I couldn't even lift my arm to get the remote to change channels on the TV. That kind of sadness and depression is as much physical as it is emotional, yet still I got up every day and went to work like nothing was going on.

I was a master at dissociating, but I must admit that at times it was a useful tool. I would never have been able to hold down a regular job without that ability to shut everything down while I went to work. In fact, work was going really well. I had moved from customer service agent, to customer service manager, to quality manager at head office in Sydney. It amazes me how I could disconnect the terrible traumas I was talking about with my therapist from my working persona. It's one of the toughest things I find today is that I've learnt NOT to disconnect the parts of myself so much, so I fall apart more easily. But still, even today I hold down a regular job and I've never had a day off for being depressed.

It had been years since I'd thought of David. I remember distinctly promising him that if I ever dealt with my shit enough to face it, that I would contact him and let him help me the rest of the way. "Let me help you, let me be by your side," I remember him saying, and I knew he meant it. David was so special to me; one of those lifetime connections that don't break no matter how much time or space separates you. I was feeling pretty good about my healing progress. I thought back to David and what he meant to me. I was older now - not so confused like I'd been when I betrayed him and ran off with abusive asshole number two, or was it three? Too many to remember. I was ready to face David, I was going to call and ask if he could help me going through my past. I had acknowledged that I couldn't heal alone and needed people in my corner. David was definitely in my corner.

Would he still be there? Would I still love him just as much as before? I was all excited at this possibility. I had it all planned. I could move in, get a job nearby and see if our soul mate connection stood the test of time. He could help me with my counselling – we could reconnect. My imagination roared with possibilities. My heart was warmed even by thinking about him. I was ready.

I called his number. I knew he wouldn't have moved; he was a static being. The phone was disconnected. *OK a hurdle, it's a small one*, I thought to myself. *I will keep track of him through his film and TV scripts, maybe call the Little Theatre where we first met to get a message to him.* Sometime later as I was scanning one of the TV shows that he wrote for, I saw "In memoriam David. Deceased Aug 29th 2001." David had died a year earlier. I looked David up on IMDB (Internet Movie Data Base) and sure enough there it was: "Deceased. Aug 29th 2001." I couldn't breathe. It was true. My soul mate was dead.

I'd let my best friend die alone. I believe he had tried to contact me, but because I was in hiding from asshole number three, I had moved around a lot and wouldn't have been easy to track down. I was devastated. Now all the problems I had run away from, came back to haunt me. Why hadn't I just stayed with David? Why had I run from the only man I ever truly loved? The worst part was I couldn't even share my pain with anyone. We had kept our relationship secret. When we had been going to marry we were going to surprise everyone, because he was a lot older than me and we didn't want the judgement of others interfering with our relationship. Now it could never happen, and my selfishness was the only thing that had stopped it.

So much for older and wiser; all I want to do is to be able to watch another sunset with him, or keep him company while he died. Having said that, I'm not sure I would have been mature enough to deal with losing my partner. I may not have survived. I lost my soul mate forever and I could never express to him how I felt, and once again I suffered in *silence*.

I wanted to visit his grave. I don't even know where he's buried – we never spoke of our relationship to anyone. It is perhaps the biggest regret of my life, and I hold pain until this day for it. It feels unresolved. I even tried to connect through mediums and although I've had signs he was around, he's never come through to speak to me. I "talk" to him often and I imagine his answers, but I find it hard to believe he hears me. At that moment, my impetus to heal came to a crashing halt. I realised how much I had taken for granted, and I knew I could never get it back. I'd never had someone who believed in me that much; not just saying they believed in me but backing it up with action. I felt stupid.

Having said that, healing-wise, it was perhaps the most powerful stage that I'd had. I was even more determined to beat this thing. So I took responsibility and held myself accountable for my mistake with love in my heart, not shame. Even though this was something unfixable because he'd died, and I didn't get to say goodbye or say what I wanted, the lesson wasn't to say it to David but to make sure the other people in my life knew their value from my perspective. I will never take a relationship like this for granted again. And I won't run away from my pain. Now that I realise the lesson, I just need an opportunity to practice it. I can't say that I have resolved this internally completely. I am still working on parts of it. Forgiveness comes up a lot, especially for myself.

The good news is that I was able to love and be loved. This means that if it had happened at all, it could happen again…but hopefully it will be with a woman next time ;-) Even after everything I'd been through, I was still able to love at this deep level. This warmed my soul, and I held onto that for the next decade and a half. I still hold onto that now. I think when I have resolved this regret, I will probably be open to finding true love again.

VICTIM'S COMPENSATION

IT WAS AFTER THE EVENT OF DAVID'S DEATH THAT THE WHEELS started to fall off. That feeling of radicalism started to emerge. It happens when you feel like you're getting close to the edge. It's a dangerous but necessary place to be. It's as if you're at boot camp and you are at what you think is your breaking point, and the closer you get to it, the more radical you feel. I was there in 2002. The seed had been planted for major change to occur. I was at a point in my counselling where I was done with the chitchat and really wanted to get my teeth into the truth of what the hell was going on with me. I was grieving David terribly and wanted to roar from the nearest mountaintop all of my pain, and all of my experiences. I had to do something different. This getting up and going to work every day and going to counselling wasn't moving me forward, and now the added pressure of losing David, even though I hadn't seen or heard from him in a while, was intense. I knew I had made a mistake staying so safe. I was in my safe little job, in my safe home town, with my safe counsellor. And I was in no way safe.

In my radical mood, I decided that I needed to do more to stand up for myself against the crime that was committed against me; the gang rape. I wasn't healing from it. I hadn't even really talked about it, so I decided to go to the police and tell them what had happened. It was quite surreal. I wasn't upset when I told them, in fact I was quite disconnected. It was like I was telling someone else's story. I had no emotion about it. I was dead inside – the glazed eyes returned. I didn't tell them the whole truth. I left out the part about my boyfriend being the initiator. I just wasn't ready to face that yet, but I told them the truth. I couldn't remember everything but weird details came back to mind as I replayed the story. It was stressful but not as bad as I thought. But it wasn't as good as I thought either, so I went one step further and applied for victim's compensation.

I don't know what I was expecting, but I was hoping for some kind of shift; an evolution of mood. As the months wore on while the police investigated I got less and less excited at the prospect of feeling any kind of relief, and then finally, a phone call. The detective called and asked to meet. We went to the café around the corner and had tea.

He said, "We've done all we can. Without more evidence the case is stayed."

That meant that unless someone from the event spontaneously confessed, nothing more would be done by the police. Still, they had proved enough of the event that they believed it was highly likely that it actually happened. That was enough to keep the victim's compensation application open.

As I sat in the café with the detective, he probably expected my usual dissociated reaction of just saying, "Ok thanks, bye!" Instead I started to cry, I was shaking – I couldn't hold my cup to my mouth. I tried to break up the emotion by cracking a joke. It didn't work. The detective then took a call and had to rush off to another emergency. I was left there alone with my thoughts of, *My life is falling apart and nothing happens to these guys!*

I was shattered. I felt like the very threads holding me together were starting to unwind, but I pushed through as I usually did. I continued with the victim's compensation application, but that was a struggle too. They lost my file; the person who was dealing with my account left and they had no record of my documents. I am talking many, many documents over a two-year period, not just a couple of forms. I had several stop-starts. I wondered if it was worth it. It didn't seem to matter any more. What once had been my radical motion towards healing just fizzled. For me to shift this huge weight I needed a huge force. I looked for new drastic measures.

One day at work we received an email with a Powerpoint presentation of all the other companies that were affiliated with the company I worked for: Ireland, Australia, the US, and Canada. I walked into the CEO's office and asked if I could go and work for the Canadian affiliate. He picked up the phone, called the CEO of the group, and said "Roe wants to go to Canada."

A few months later, once my visa application was processed, I was on a plane to Canada after selling my car and all my stuff. I moved to Montreal. I got on the plane on Dec 14[th,] 2005 in forty-degree heat and

I got off the plane a day or so later in Montreal at -22 degrees. It was a shock to the system. Sitting on the plane I actually felt a boost in my mood. I was excited at the prospect of my new life. I thought about the trip itself as a journey away from my trauma, and I felt like I was being reborn in a way. I loved the country, I loved the city, the snow, and the people, and I had a blast becoming "Canadian." And thus began my Canadian journey.

I still had the compensation application in the background, but it became a less important battle and was even harder to manage from another country. I was distracted now with all the change happening in my life. In fact, when I received the compensation it was thousands of dollars and having struggled financially for most of my life you'd think I would have been grateful. But I wasn't. It was 2006 before I received it, four years after I'd first applied. I felt nothing. I paid a few debts and intended to pay all of them, but then I had this resistance. I was getting more and more depressed thinking of all this money coming in and then going straight back out again to pay debts like it had never been there in the first place. I felt like at least I should buy a couple of things. I wanted something to show for my struggles through life due to the rape. So I put a deposit on a house and bought a car and a trip back to Aus and a computer. None of which I still have. That whole victim's compensation process did very little to help me heal. I should have kept going and paid all my debts so I could start a fresh new life and buy the house and car later. It would have been much smarter, but I was making decisions coloured by trauma and emotion. I wasn't being mindful of what would truly help me heal. I just wanted to feel better in the moment. It's easy now to look back in hindsight at my mistake and see it so clearly, but at the time I was impatient. I thought that the depression meant I was on the wrong path. I know now that it meant I was exactly where I was supposed to be. I would change none of these things and certainly wouldn't want them erased by not having experienced the victim compensation process. It just didn't provide the healing I thought it would.

THE UP-SIDE

All was not lost, my victim's compensation has been a very significant aspect of my journey. It provided me with the $10,000 I needed to become a Canadian citizen. It gave me a trip back to Australia to see my stepdad for the last time, and it let me live in my own little house for a year and a half and enabled me to get my dog.

More importantly, the victim's compensation process gave me perhaps one of the most intrinsic validations I have ever had. Without this experience I may not have healed at all. It was very important to acknowledge the impact that my gang rape experience had on my life. To apply for compensation I had to write a victim-impact statement. This was a highly successful exercise for me to identify just what I had lost. Dissociation makes you ignore the reality of how much something has impacted you. To heal you have to acknowledge it all. It was a mindful moment to really get down to examine how this experience, and those abusive experiences that had come before it, had affected my life. Not only was I able to identify it for myself, but it would also be seen by a panel of high authorities, including a judge. This statement formed the foundation of my compensation case. When that came back positive it meant that the higher laws of the land had deemed my victim impact to be worthy of some compensation. It wasn't about the money for me. This was about being totally truthful about how these negative events had altered my life. It was an official validation. Sure my counsellors had validated me before, but this was much more official. Not only that, I was able to give a voice to what these events meant to me and my life. They had devastated me. They had changed my life forever.

This picture was taken on the day I received word that my victim's compensation case was approved and I would receive a significant amount of money. This was my alleged "happy face."

THE CANADIAN DREAM

I LOVED CANADA. I LOVED LIVING HERE, AND WORKING HERE but it had its challenges. The job was the same but the way people approached it was totally different. In Australia, I was the glue that bound together all the systems for all departments. I had both the vision and strategy to pull it all together and to implement some great processes to make the business flow more smoothly and efficiently. In Canada, I had the same job with the same company structure but no one wanted to be glued together to work for a common goal. That was an alien concept here. Here it was every department for themselves and no goals matched. I worked on a project for two years and then because IT didn't want to build the supporting reports, I had to drop it.

So the distraction of Canada started to wane and the heavy emotions returned. I was jaded for sure, and I let that emanate from me at work. I complained about everything. My inner turbulence had revisited and once again the radicals came out. I decided to try a live-in PTSD program. It was a great program and helped a lot, but it too upturned my life. I came out fighting and strong but the integration with the real world faded pretty quickly, and soon I was back in corporate-land where I had started. I couldn't quite work out the balance between living authentically and existing in the real world where much of it is a game. We put on our happy faces and push through to get ahead. Even relationships were challenged. I had a choice to adopt the new ways and lose my boyfriend and friends, or to hold onto what was around me and go back to not being mindful, not acknowledging my true self, and stuffing everything back in the corner. I had forgotten the tools I learned in the program and pushed aside my feelings again so that I could be a normal person for a while, with a job and a house and a car and a dog. The healing I'd claimed for myself during the program was still valuable but just not practiced at this time.

I lost my passion and my job. Then I had to move cities to get work and I ended up in Ottawa, still searching for myself. Although I finally figured out I was gay, I was nowhere near living an authentic life. On a positive note, I made really good friends in Montreal; some I still communicate with now, so it wasn't a total washout. I relished Montreal as a city to live in, but paying the bills pushed me to the neighbouring province of Ontario where the Canadian capital, Ottawa became my new home. My emotion-stained and inauthentic thinking led to erratic decisions, and continued to create negative consequences.

I E.M.P.O.W.E.R.
HEAL KIT INITIATIVE 6 - EVOLUTION

~ "The requirements for our evolution have changed. Survival is no longer sufficient. Our evolution now requires us to develop spiritually - to become emotionally aware and make responsible choices. It requires us to align ourselves with the values of the soul - harmony, cooperation, sharing, and reverence for life." ~ **GARY ZUKAV**

ALL THE INITIATIVES UP UNTIL NOW ARE A LEAD-UP TO THIS MAIN point. If you want your evolution to be a true revolution in your healing, then pay attention to this initiative. Every other stage is intrinsic, however, this initiative is the pivotal one. When I said, expand your thinking, you must especially test that in this phase. When I said, use your mindfulness to deal with the emotional roller coaster that ensues, now is the time when the proverbial shit will hit the fan. Every initiative is tested.

ACCESSING THE DEEP BELIEFS - PROOF OF LIFE

MY BELIEF IS THAT WE COME INTO THE WORLD PURE WITH OUR pure energy and all its personality traits, innate abilities, and structures including our human knowledge. I believe that how we react to the world is also pre-set. For example, I am sensitive to energy and to people, and things can overwhelm me. Even at forty-eight years old, sometimes I need quiet, meditation, or a nature walk to hear my own thoughts and feelings as I am so influenced and affected by all that's going on around me. I have been like this since birth.

Then, once we come into the world, we experience our first years. We are like sponges; we absorb everything around us, good and bad, and the way we interpret the world in these early years will determine how we view the world later. You don't have to look too hard to find the concept that we learn our core beliefs between the ages of birth to seven. The documentary series *Seven Up!* captures it nicely. It tracks the lives of fourteen children every seven years, right through to their fifties, and possibly beyond if they keep going. Its basic premise is based on Francis Xavier's quote, "Give me a child until he is seven and I will give you the man."

Recently I added to this concept that we then spend the rest of our lives trying to "prove" our initial theories of how we could interact with the world, unless we consciously interrupt the patterns. Now I've heard that concept before too. It's not original and certainly not mine, but something about the way Paul Ekman says it in his book *Emotions Revealed* made it click for me. He says, "When we are gripped by an inappropriate emotion, we interpret what is happening in a way that fits with how we are feeling and we ignore our knowledge that doesn't fit."

This steered me toward thinking that just like a theoretical proof, I had been using the core feelings like a belief statement such as "I am worthless," that I'd learnt when I was five years old, and then I have gone about proving why that is true. "I am worthless, I am invisible, nothing I say or do alters the negative consequences that happen to me. I have no control over anything, and trust no one." I have spent the last forty-something years reinforcing and proving these theories. At five years old, that's all I had the capacity to understand. I am being hit by my caregiver, so I must be bad. We certainly can't differentiate between bad behaviour and being bad, especially when everything else in our environment confirms our "badness."

I call it our "Proof of Life." Deepak Chopra calls it mental conditioning. We prove our life theories over and over not realising that the original statement is wrong, misguided, and developed from the perspective of a five-year-old. How can it possibly be accurate, when we developed it at a time that our brains can't yet comprehend complex thinking? It doesn't take a genius to work it out that our five-year old's perspective is skewed and unrealistic, yet how many of us (myself included) live by our original statement and prove it beyond reasonable doubt? I am guilty of this for sure.

I know that "proof of life" means something entirely different. It's a term used to prove that hostages are still alive so that the hostage takers can negotiate, but I feel this is somewhat appropriate, given that we are held hostage by our five-year-old's perception of the world. When we are five our lives depend on figuring out how to interact with our caregivers. We work out theories in order to get the life-saving care we need. To rescue ourselves from our five-year-old concepts we need to debunk our original theories and remove their power using adult thinking and beliefs. Otherwise our view of the world is skewed by what original statements we are proving, and every time we have an inappropriate emotion, we just ignore that which doesn't fit our proof.

In my job loss due to being bullied at work, my initial instinct was to say that even when I do the right thing and stand up and take care of myself, I am still the only one being affected negatively. I am the one out on the street wondering where I'm going to get the money to pay my rent and nothing happens to the perpetrator. The business I worked at was not affected in the slightest. Not only was I without a job, but I had been left emotionally exhausted. I didn't even feel I could work after that for quite a few months at least.

There will always be a way to spin my circumstances to prove my negative beliefs. I can leave stuff out, take it out of context, or ignore the positive to focus on the one thing that proves my negative approach. And the smarter I get the better I get at proving my theory. I am so smart I could turn any situation around to fit into my belief. I was proving the theories of a five-year-old. You know, for a smart lady I can be pretty dumb sometimes! Even when I had a realisation, an AHA! Moment, and I would temporarily suspend my depression, it would always return because I became so damn good at proving otherwise. So much so, that it wasn't even conscious. Even when I had that moment of clarity after leaving my wife and I felt so awesome for letting go of something that wasn't working, the depression soon returned, because the belief wasn't shattered - how could it be? I didn't know the "worthlessness" core belief existed.

The only thing I have found in my life so far amongst all my tricks and tools to shift that depression has been to understand that I was proving my life as I knew it when I was a small child. As it does for everyone, the proof of my very existence depended on how well I proved my theory. As children, we are trying to find our places in the world; how we relate to it, and we interpret the things that happen in relation to us. My father beat us as children even before we could entertain thought; before we could rationalise and cognitively figure out why he was doing this. And we assigned meaning to how we felt and why. As a young child, you don't know anything else but you, so everything relates to that. Our psychological development is only up to egocentrism at that point. So, if children are beaten their only reaction is to think that they are responsible.

My belief is that our very existence depends on us "proving" our existence by understanding how we fit in. This bares the theory that we deserve being beaten and we are worth nothing. It does not matter what our theory is - as long as we have one and it makes sense. From that point forward we reinforce the idea by viewing the world and seeing how it fits with our theory, rather than viewing what happens in our later lives and devising a theory from that.

In other words, to dispel this feeling, and to turn my life around, I needed to not only come up with new statements, and actively go about proving them, but I had to practice them regularly to turn them into beliefs. That took time. I could see my resilience, my strength, and my integrity but I always have, and if I didn't deliberately take a different look at my reality to incorporate the new beliefs, the negative beliefs bounced back. I needed to form new habits and that took commitment. In psychology this is called re-framing.

In this example of leaving work, if I expand my thinking I can see that all I lost was a job that was sucking the life out of me. It called into question my integrity every day I stepped over the threshold of the front door. I took a hit on my spiritual bank account, and the longer it went on, the bigger the withdrawal on my emotional life. It was literally killing me to the point where I was about to check into a hospital and put myself on suicide watch. It's never a bad thing to lose a job that makes you feel like that. No job is worth my life. I either needed to change my reaction to work or leave. I had tried many times to change my reaction to it - but to no avail. You can't change others, only yourself, and at some point - if you still can't cope with it - it's time to go. My life was worth more than that. That was my expanded reality. I had just proven my worth, disintegrating my previous belief system and revealing that I do have power. And even though I was unemployed for a while, once I recovered physically and emotionally, I did have a positive outcome. I found the job I am in now at the furniture company. So after some time I proved that I do make a difference on my outcomes.

ABANDONMENT THEORY

I was alone and no one came to my rescue during the gang rape or even earlier back through my childhood. I was abandoned by my family, my boyfriend, and by God.

DEBUNKED - I had the strength to survive horrible traumas all by myself. I proved to myself that I must have incredible resilience, intelligence, mindfulness, and stamina to get through such tremendous physical, mental, emotional, and spiritual violence against me. I AM A WARRIOR! I can trust and rely on myself for anything in life. Had family, friends, or police intervened I may never have known just how much strength I have. No force on earth can take away my experiences. They are proof of how powerful I am as an individual. Was I abandoned? Maybe! And maybe there are just times in our lives where we need to prove to ourselves who we are. It appears that I am independent, determined, and spirited without the need to rely on others during the hardest moments of my life, so I can get through anything at this point.

The gang rape was the worst moment of my life, but the worst wasn't the rape itself, it was the fact that no one had come to my rescue. That haunted me for some time and I can go deep into that feeling, but in fact, this is my strength. Who I am now is built on the "me" that survived, entirely without interference from the support of others. This proves my independence at its purest essence. I didn't need help from anyone. I can use this moment as the best I can ever be. And I could only have been alone to do it.

WORTHLESSNESS THEORY

My life has no meaning if I don't turn my negative experiences into something good, like the mother who lost a child to a drunk driver and now goes and gives talks at schools. I am doing nothing with my bad experiences, no one will read this book, I am not valued as an employee or girlfriend, and even my friends don't care enough to call on my birthday.

DEBUNKED - My life has meaning because of my experiences. I am no angel but I live my life with integrity and good intentions that aren't always met…but I try. I try to be better every day. I hold down a decent job, I give back to the community through volunteer work. My life already has meaning within it - so much. My story documented here is meaningful just because I AM. I'm glad I didn't go down the drugs and alcohol path, not because it's wrong, but because it's so much harder to recover when toxins are also interfering with thinking clearly. I have enough emotional toxins to blur the edges of life already. I didn't turn violent although I can easily see how I could have. There's so much anger and rage caused by my traumas that it wouldn't be any wonder if I did, but something stopped me. Who I am stopped me from turning into the very people I abhor. I broke the chain, stopped the cycle - that's meaningful enough in itself.

There's meaning in what I went through in relation to how I overcame it. I have proven that humanity can survive and prosper after such events. If I can do it then anyone can. I am no great person and I have no special powers. I just chose never to give up and to find peace for myself. It's not like I feel great every day, but that journey is worthy too. I don't need to "do" anything else to prove my worth - it already exists. I simply need to open my heart and embrace it. I am here, and I am able to express myself and how I view my experiences in words. What greater meaning is there for me than that? Sure, I could give talks to young women to help them prevent some of the situations I found myself in. I could talk to people with trauma who have tried everything to heal and can't quite get there, and maybe my experiences will help them. But I don't need that to find meaning in my life. It's already there.

I used to wish that I had died during the gang rape, then my murdered body would have had significant meaning, and the truth would have been revealed as it was. Outpourings of grief and what I meant to all who knew me at the time would have flooded in, without me to witness it. Why did it happen and how would all have been revealed? Who did what and who didn't? I would have then known that my life had meaning, however, I would have only known in spirit, for a life I no longer had. Now, at forty-five-plus years old I have so much more. I still have my life; I have had twenty-five more years of meaning. I can now write this book to illuminate my story, so that those who need to see it can see meaning in their own lives. For some reason, if you survive you're not supposed to talk about it. So there will be people who say, "Why did she have to put 'that' in there and be so graphic?" Well the answer is because that is my story. It happened to me, so the least you can do is read it. Had I actually died during the gang rape there would have been no question about displaying my story everywhere, watching it all unfold on the news or in documentaries on forensics, but somehow, if the person actually survives we have a hard time reading it. We put the book down and go and watch *Game of Thrones!* Or *The Walking Dead*. No one seems to question that kind of violence.

This time I won't be silent. Here I am sharing my story. It has even greater meaning that I survived and lived my life; albeit a different life from the one I had before my experiences. The truth is that seeking a "greater meaning" in my life by way of doing something momentous like being a paramedic or in victim services, or an emergency manager, or other such vocation is merely another avoidance tactic. I do not need a specific vocation or activity to make my life meaningful - it simply is, especially because of what I have already been through, rather than what I do next. I am enough.

UNLOVABLE THEORY

I am not lovable. I should go after any sign of love I can as I will never get any more, and I will ignore all signs that the love is toxic or unhealthy, because at least it provides something. No one will ever love me for who I am as I am too damaged and weird and intense.

DEBUNKED - I must learn to love myself. No one else matters, however, I will find love in many different forms and places, and I don't need to put up with toxic relationships to get it. I can let go of little pieces of love to wait for real, comprehensive love. I already have the love of friends; it will only be a matter of time before I meet another soul mate like David.

I don't know what would have happened with David. It may have fallen apart once I realised I was gay, but I know this for sure - he loved me wholeheartedly. Of course, I couldn't accept it at the time - it didn't fit my proof of life, but now my expanded thinking can include the reality that he loved me unconditionally, and I was more messed up then than I am now. Now I've had the benefit of years of counselling and work on myself. So, if he could love me in that shattered state, it's possible for someone to find me lovable in this state. But I can't expect anyone to love me if I don't love myself. I can't say I've conquered this yet, but I am looking every day for evidence to support this new, recreated proof of my life. Instead of feeling like I'm weird and intense, I can think of it as rich with texture. I'm certainly not boring. Lol. I used to think, *Who could ever love this broken being?* Now I believe that my brokenness is my strength. I have seen it all and opened up to great vulnerability, so my capacity for intimacy is greater. And I want to be with someone who loves me for that very reason.

UNWISE WITH MONEY THEORY

I am terrible with money. I do not deserve abundance. Money is dirty and should be feared. I chose a company that actively proved this theory for me. For a year, I had been hounded by my boss about not meeting an impossible budget, set unfairly and unrealistically. Yet my branch had over forty percent greater revenue and made eighty percent more profit than the previous year. I had chosen a company whose belief system reflected my own about money. No wonder I couldn't leave. It supported my proof of life belief that I was bad with money and didn't know how to manage it. That's a powerful belief to have kept me bound to a job that I didn't like. It's weird because as much as I didn't like the situation, I never seemed to be able to get out of it, because I didn't realise I had this subconscious connection to it that was stronger than my conscious thinking. Had I not interrupted the flow of this thinking I may never have gotten out of my bad situations.

DEBUNKED - I am excellent with money. Yes, I am bankrupt, I had insurmountable debt, and I made decisions that negatively affected me financially. But Donald Trump has been bankrupt more than once. I left the company that was telling me how bad I was with money, because I believed they were wrong. I brought in forty percent more revenue than the previous year. That's the truth. When I directed theatre productions, they tended to be the most lucrative the companies I worked for had ever had. I did not overspend on costs, I made cuts without harming people, and in all of the businesses with which I have been associated, I have either saved greatly for them or improved their revenue. Even speaking personally, though I had been maxed out with debt for some time, I still managed to have an almost AAA credit rating because I always paid my bills on time - right up to the day before my bankruptcy. After that I had to let it all go. With most of my income pouring out the door to cover my overwhelming debts, I managed to live quite frugally for many years.

I tried hard to get out from under the debt, but when you have a strong, subconscious belief that you are constantly trying to prove, it decides every turning point for you. As much as you try - you break your boundaries and say yes to people you really could have said no to. In my case, just when it started to turn around I would do something (not deliberately but subconsciously) to sabotage it. It's not like I was out buying sports cars and expensive trips and jewellery. I was usually saying yes to my partner when I could have said, no, I can't afford it.

I could have sat down with all of my ex-partners and specifically discussed money and who was going to pay what and how. I could have made it a deal breaker if they didn't agree with fairness and what I believed I could pay. But I didn't, and now that I am conscious of my underlying sabotage, I can stop it. The next time a financially affected decision comes into play, I will assess it using my recreated proof of life. I am great with money and deserve abundance and the ability to live a comfortable lifestyle. I am not responsible for other people's money issues, either physical or emotional, and I won't be sucked into their stuff just because I love them. If it's real love - they can work with me to sit down and figure out a financial plan that works for both of us.

Had I sat down with my wife and discussed finances before we moved in together, I would have realised that our ideals were incompatible and we wouldn't have been able to resolve these issues. And if you can't deal with your finances in a relationship, the rest of it doesn't look good. I would have split up with her then; I would have been truthful with myself, and although it would have hurt, it would have been better off for both of us in the long run. I just wasn't there yet. I needed more growing.

UNHAPPY LIFE THEORY

It has been my belief for a long time that I have led an unhappy life and that I always will. This belief, unlike the others, came a bit later in life. It is a consequence of one of the core beliefs. People can't believe they are not enough all their lives and be happy at the same time.

This belief feels harder to break; maybe because of its distance from the core beliefs. I look at other people's lives and wonder how they get it so easy. I know everyone has their trials, but when I add up all of mine they seem to be more intrusive in my life than I see in other people's lives. Other people seem happy. They had great childhoods with Mom and Dad, as teens they hung out with cool friends in cool places, and as adults they are together, and in great jobs. They have houses and families and are generally happy.

For me as a child, I didn't know any different, so I felt happy despite the constant feeling that I needed to be better. Ultimately I was happy. Kids are existential – they live in the moment. Still, there were already signs early on that something was affecting me. When I got lightly tapped on the butt by a teacher in first grade when I was about seven, I burst into tears and wet my pants. I was terrified and it didn't even hurt. Even so, if you asked me back then how I felt, I would have said and believed that I was happy.

While all these negatives were being created, there I was – feeling "happy" and almost totally oblivious to reality. We are born with peace. I came into the world with an assumption that I was happy. I hadn't yet learned how to look at my life dimly. My ignorance gave me a grace period, but it soon faded. After repeated episodes of my father's rage I started to grasp unhappiness, and by teenagehood it turned into full-on depression. As always though, I was still high-functioning. I still had good experiences, but at home I either played piano to escape my world or I would stare at the fire for hours. By early adulthood my life was already completely upside down after spending four years with Peter including the gang rape. It only went downhill after that.

DEBUNKED- So how do I view this one in a different light? I can't deny that I was unhappy from about the age of ten - it is a fact. So I need to look at the future and the present. This belief feels harder to break. With the other beliefs, the answers came to me easily, as if they were already there and I just needed to shine a light on them. This one I had to think about. The truth is, I had been very unhappy for a long time, but is everyone else so opposite? If you look at why Oprah is so popular; it stems from the fact that so many people are unhappy with their lives and are looking for more out of them. Tony Robbins has excellent success at his "Date with Destiny" workshops every year. If everyone was as happy as I thought they were, then these things wouldn't be so successful.

In attempts to stave off my unhappiness, even for a while, I have made bad decisions, so how can I look at my life and say that I am currently happy and that I will be happy in the future? I can't change my past. I have had innumerable experiences that were exceptionally traumatic; the effects of which are long lasting. Well the answer is, I do the same as I do for the other beliefs. I look for proof that I am happy in my present, and if I am happy at that time, then the possibility exists that I can remain so for my future.

After I'd left my job, I'd been off work for over a month and I had done things every day that made me feel good. I hardly missed a day of hiking with my dog - one of my favourite things. I didn't have to force myself to get up and go to work at a company with which I had integrity issues. I lived in a beautiful area surrounded by spectacular scenery and nature that I love. But even all that was not enough to raise my mood level to "happy." It had to come from a deeper place. I've always done positive things that make me feel good, but the feelings soon faded. I had to get at that misguided belief to shift my mood up a notch or two to feel true joy.

Now I already know that what you focus on expands, but I also know that empty affirmations telling myself that life is good are never going to make it so, because I simply don't believe it. I don't believe in the "fake it 'til you make it" philosophy. Affirmations will only ever be a temporary fix for me if I don't access the cause of my discontent. Otherwise it's like going to the chiropractor and getting your back adjusted but the muscles surrounding your spine are still tense, so as soon as you walk out the door and hop into your car, the first bump you roll over will readjust your spine to the way the muscles are pulling it. It won't take much. If you release the muscles and then get adjusted – the adjustment will last, because there's no force pulling the spine out of place again. Affirmations for me are just like that. I can fake it for a while, but it's not going to stick because there's too much force pulling it in another direction.

So how did I reach happiness? Especially seeing as my life really did suck after I left my job? I couldn't pay my rent the following week, I didn't have any money for food, it was very stressful. I didn't have a job and I would have preferred to be in a loving relationship. I would have preferred a Christmas spent with loved ones. All I did was stay at home, go hiking with my dog, and feel really depressed.

However - and here's the kicker - it was the most real Christmas I'd ever had. No bullshit. And in fact, I was invited to dinner with friends but I didn't want a pity invite. I preferred my actual reality of not having many true friends close by in my life at that time. I didn't have to sit around with a family I have nothing in common with. I didn't have to put on my fake happy face for friends that I only kind of have a superficial connection with, and nothing could have made me happier. I had finally found my authentic self, whether that self was sad, depressed, stressed about no income, angry, loving, happy, or whatever - it was authentic. Happiness can ONLY come from being real. And as I allowed myself to be totally real in that crappy situation, I'd never felt happier. I would only build it from there.

No affirmation or life circumstance will create happiness unless I am being true to me. That is where I went wrong with Angie. I was not true to me from the start. The same with my job at the training centre. I knew from the start who they were and what they were pretending to be, and I knew it was incongruous with who I was. Yet I took it anyway - no wonder it ended up where it did. Happiness cannot be built on denial.

I could have done with some money to pay my rent of course, but even that is real. I was motivated to find a great job that suited my skills and values and didn't reinforce old beliefs, but instead supported my recreated ones. I was happy with my authentic self, whichever mood it was in. I loved it because I had never allowed myself to be authentic except when I was a child and hadn't yet learned NOT to be. Children have a great way of being real. I remember saying to someone as a child, "Why do you look so fat?" to a pregnant woman. Lol. I guess tact doesn't really come into it. I would love to be that radically truthful, but I can tone it down a bit. At least children are real. And we should teach them how to manage it rather than how to suppress it.

SHAME THEORY

I am ashamed of who I am and of what I have done. I have many regrets that cannot be undone. I made bad choices by believing I was not empowered.

DEBUNKED - True clearing the slate means existing with whatever happened. Even in my worst trauma of life I still have empowered choices. Regret is just something that warns you what not to do next time. If you didn't regret the mistake – you would probably repeat it. I had sex with people I didn't want to, I rejected my best friend David to go out with abusive men, I have done really dumb things so that I would be loved by a partner, including going out with them when I knew in my heart it was wrong for me. I still scratch my head in wonder at how the hell I could have made these conscious decisions; these terrible decisions that had dire consequences in my life. How can I forgive myself for these things? How can I release the shame and embarrassment?

This is a tough one, and yet the answer is quite simple. I need to step up for these things and accept them as part of who I am. I can go into excuses that many counsellors have provided me, such as how I didn't know better or that I learned this behaviour from my devastating past, but the truth is I made bad choices. Any situation I have been in; my finances, the house, the gang rape, the abusive boyfriends, the failed marriages have all been the result of bad decisions I made…mixed with predators looking for vulnerable victims, which I was. I don't hold myself responsible for the abusive actions of others. However, I could have left Peter at the phone call, or any time in the next three years when he presented abusive behaviour, especially after I found out his plans, but I didn't. And that's what I have to take responsibility for - because if I don't I will always give away my power and I will continue to ignore that I can make good decisions to make my life much better. If I acknowledge what my part is in my past, I can make a better future. You can't change what you don't acknowledge. So as much I can see my previous counsellors' points of how other forces impacted my decision making, I can also see where I do have power and how I can make sure that I never make those mistakes again. I'm not shaming myself and saying it's all my fault – it isn't. I am just saying that in what seems like hopeless times there is empowerment. I can make better decisions. I can choose not to focus on my misgivings and instead choose what is right for me and those around me. The positive consequences will naturally follow, and I must let go of the outcome and wait for them to flow.

It doesn't matter if you have had the worst trauma in the world, there are things you can't change but there are choices you can make in your life that will be more positive. It may be that you have to accept a new reality or viewpoint, but the benefits of healing are worth it.

Even in my marriage to Angie I had doubts in the first weeks of us dating; doubts that turned out to be valid and ultimately what separated us in the end. Had I been honest with myself and with Angie, I could have saved us both all of that heartache. I don't regret that either. I had great experiences with Angie as well; ones that I wouldn't want to wish away. It's important to acknowledge without shame and blame. We all make mistakes – it's part of life, but we also must own our part in them even if there are other factors involved and there usually are. I did not have a choice with my father, that is certain. But at nineteen with the gang rape, I played a part even if it was heavily influenced by prior experiences.

All of my mistakes have one thing in common. They all related to seeking the love and approval of others to whom I was emotionally attached, and if I don't own up to that now, I will continue to make similar mistakes. Even the house situation came about from my strong emotional attachment, due to it being bought with funds from my victim's compensation. I was so emotionally connected to it that when I could have sold the house I didn't, because I couldn't let go of the attachment. I was trying to fill a void that was unfillable. And now I need to acknowledge this void, accept my actions, and cut myself a break. I have already done my time in my emotional prisons. I don't need to keep berating myself. I almost suffered the death penalty. I don't think I need to serve any more time.

I am no different from anyone else with their shame, their regrets, their mistakes. We ALL have them. It's what I do next that will determine whether I have learned from these mistakes or not. I need to remain true to me in the face of unhealthy emotional attachment in the future even if it hurts, because I will have to give up something to stay true to myself. But the benefits will be far better than anything I could gain from holding onto void-filling in an unfillable black hole.

The point here is if you are doing something you know is wrong: STOP! Get help of some description even if it's just advice from a trusted friend. You can delude yourself into thinking, it's ok, it's only affecting me, but that's not true. Your life touches so many others. Even if it's just in your mood or inappropriate anger, you indirectly affect others. Also if it's affecting you negatively, that's enough to say it's not ok and to stop doing whatever it is.

Now every time I crave approval from others or I want a relationship, or I want someone to love me, I stop and ask myself why I am feeling the lack of love. I am enough just as I am, with all of my past bad choices, needing no one else to validate me, and if I am fearful that I won't be validated, that's even more reason to just feel the feelings and allow them to exist. Do not act on the fear because it will create the wrong environment. It's enough for me to believe I am enough, just as I am, right now.

These are just examples of how to debunk your 5 year old's theories, I have many more, but you get the picture. You can choose to view anything in your life as supportive of you healing or supportive of your old skewed theories. I choose to be open to the new theories. You don't even have to believe them at first, you just have to be open to them. Then your evolution will be a revolution in your life.

FORTY-FIED

I FELT SOMETHING SHIFT AT FORTY-FIVE. MY BODY STARTED TO change, my wisdom increased, and my patience for bullshit decreased. I just felt like I was getting too old to put up with people's crap, but in a good way. Now I know why there's a stereotype of grumpy old men. They just don't want to put up with the bullshit anymore. Time's a wasting!

My body started to slow down considerably. Up to forty-five, I could run three times a week and lose weight easily without really modifying my eating - not so after forty-five. My eyes needed glasses for reading, and I could no longer eat pizza or fatty foods without some major consequences, but this is where I really started to feel like I *got* life. The penny dropped. When I was learning French it all sounded foreign, and then one day it suddenly made sense. I didn't have to think so hard what the conjugation was, I didn't have to translate everything in my head back to English, I was even dreaming in French. That's what I felt when I hit forty-five. I suddenly "got" life! I "got" healing, I "got" what I was doing or not doing that was impacting my rate of healing. It's also when I finally figured out what I wanted to be when I grew up. It wasn't so important about the title or even the type of job. I just needed a job where I could use my skills, be appreciated for what I could do, and be paid reasonably for it. I didn't need to be saving the world. I even contemplated giving up writing the book because I just felt like I had been doing it for the wrong reasons. I felt like I needed to turn my negative into a positive, but ultimately I don't *have* to do that anymore. My simple steps of following my own healing initiative already turned my negative to a positive. I had already come to accept my experiences and integrate them. Sure, I still have stuff to work on but so does everyone. I am at "normalcy" now.

Even though I have suffered significant trauma, I don't feel I need to tell the world about it for me to find some meaning so that I can reduce my suffering. I have already reduced it by taking these healing initiatives. That thought actually confronted me and I felt depressed because I had thought that my own motivation for writing this book had been to do something with my trauma and make it mean something, but in my expanded thinking I realised that I already had done something. I had taken a personal journey of discovery and walked through the depths of humanity to find where I fit in. So now I am writing this book for myself, and the potential outcome of it helping others will just help me validate my experiences. The wisdom I found was just to integrate my own experience and be ok with it. This book for me is a reflection of me while being my opportunity to change the world. This is my stamp, my footprint of who I am. My writing it is less about needing to help or rescue others than it is to express myself, and just that difference will probably mean others will feel more connected to my story. It is innately human. I felt that as content as I am in my job, it's not enough for me. I need to express my deeper thoughts. I needed to connect to the world, and share my voice and be a part of humanity on the planet. Trauma had made me separate from this. Now I am back. During the gang rape I felt part of me separated and broke. I felt it almost physically, and for the subsequent years I felt disconnected to life somehow. Living through this healing journey has brought me home.

I will always write. Whether it be a blog or a book or whatever, I am a writer, and I like to share my little thoughts about the world. Ever since I was a kid I had super curiosity like wanting to see what was at the end of the rain. I wrote a blog about my experiences moving country from Sydney, Australia to Montreal, Canada and noticed life as it passed by, connecting me with life and sharing my bond with others. I will continue to do that. My depression lifted as soon as I figured out *how* I wanted to connect with the world. I realised that my connection got broken during my several traumatic experiences. It took me until I was forty-five to reconnect it. That may sound a little sad but some people never get to connect it back.

RHEUMATOLOGY – IT'S IN THE GENES

"WAIT! WHAT?" SITTING IN THE RHEUMATOLOGIST'S OFFICE I was prepared for the usual, "I don't know what the problem is, take these pills and go see a physio / chiropractor / acupuncturist, and get a few MRIs / CT scans / X-rays." I have had back pain for years; maybe fifteen to twenty, maybe more. I have tried every possible treatment: Chiropractors saying that I just need to go three times a week, then taper it off. Acupuncturists saying just come twice a week. Naturopaths telling me which vitamins I am deficient in. And physios just getting me walking again. When my back goes. . . it goes. I am on the floor, down for the count, and unless I am administered strong drugs, where I land is where I must stay. I can usually manoeuvre my way across the floor to get to a toilet but that's about it. Usually I can't get on a bed. I can't really eat from that position and it's painful. All the tests come back clear and off I go again until the next episode (often between six to twelve months apart.) It is often stress-related so no one usually pays much attention. But things have been getting worse in the last twelve months. You just know yourself and that something is wrong. But even so I was still in denial even sitting in the rheumatologist's office. So then he hit me with it. "You have ankylosing spondylitis and fibromyalgia (which I suspected) and you test positive for lupus." Well that covers all bases then, doesn't it? Ankylosing spondylitis is basically arthritis of the spine, fibromyalgia means my muscles and joints are painful, and lupus usually affects the organs. The only thing I left out was my brain although the consequences of all these things give me memory problems, lack of sleep, and extreme fatigue, so like I said – all bases covered. Ok I did freak out a little bit. I was always afraid I would end up like my mother; wake up one day and not be able to walk, have great difficulty doing simple things, and probably end up in a wheelchair some of the time like her. I couldn't go back to work that day, so I went home and just thought about my future. I had to expand my thinking a little. My new reality now included significant health issues. But once I adopted TIEWIN (this is exactly what I need) I realised that all I was doing was accepting the reality that already existed. As I said, I have had these problems for years. I have had many times where I've woken up and couldn't walk. So there's nothing really that I have to get upset about. In fact, the diagnosis will now help me get the proper treatment so I won't be in constant pain. And perhaps the relief from pain will help me sleep better and think clearer, and it may even give me back some of the lost mobility I've been experiencing over the last several years. This is a good thing!!! The fact that I went through my own healing process, made my trip from devastating to acceptance very fast. I still had to be mindful of the feelings that came up, but once I accepted reality, I was quite excited about my future with proper treatment. After fifteen to twenty years of Band-Aids, I finally get the real deal! Awesome! Not to mention, finally some validation of me saying "Something in my body is wrong."

That doesn't make it easier living with an autoimmune disease. It has impacted my daily life significantly. Simple tasks like opening a bottle or using my computer mouse are both painful and difficult now. Weekends are often spent recuperating after my short doggie hike. They used to be ten kilometres long, now they're a painful two to three kilometers with many rest stops. I was in pain every day from my diagnosis forward. After a while, though, you don't feel the pain as much, as your brain adapts to ignoring the signals. Unfortunately, because your brain is so focused on the ignoring, it makes you less able to think clearly and short-term memory fades into oblivion.

Hopefully one day soon I will find the right mix of medication to get into remission even for a while. Until then I commend anyone who is going through the same thing. I see now how hard it would have been for my mother forty-something years ago when she first saw signs of her autoimmune disease, which they now believe is the same as mine. It must have been very difficult living with an autoimmune disorder back in those days, with three children, an abusive husband, and a community who knew little about the disease. Just the fatigue alone that is produced by the illness is enough of a struggle without the pain. I wish I had seen this incredible strength in my mom earlier; it would have helped me understand my past more accurately. It's never too late though.

So that's life in my forties. My eyes are failing like most other forty-five-somethings, my body is inflamed, and life is bringing so much clarity. Even in my approach to my exercise, I have swapped my cycling shoes for a yoga mat, and I am taking right action for what my body can and can't do. Even that is new for me…all this connecting with how I really feel and matching my lifestyle to truly support it. Yes it would have been nice to have this clarity sooner in life, however, I love my forties. I can't wait to get to the wisdom of my fifties!

Mum aged seventy-five looking out from the West Vancouver seawall from her wheelchair, which we often now fight over about who's going to sit it in it.

I E.M.P.O.W.E.R.
HEAL KIT INITIATIVE 7
- RESOURCES

~ "Our uniqueness, our individuality, and our life experience moulds us into fascinating beings. I hope we can embrace that. I pray we may all challenge ourselves to delve into the deepest resources of our hearts to cultivate an atmosphere of understanding, acceptance, tolerance, and compassion. We are all in this life together." ~ **Linda Thompson**

THIS IS LIKE YOUR TOOLBOX WITH THE DIFFERENT-SHAPED HEADS to fit the other initiatives. It's whatever you choose to put in it, which you collect along the way that aids your healing. Some people have those huge tool boxes with every half-step size difference and the Swiss Army knife style with every possible shaped accessory, and others make do with a few key resources and it does the job for them.

For me, I like meditation. It may not be a traditional approach, as I can meditate while walking in the forest or sitting by the ocean. It calms me, and the more I do it - the more it helps each and every step. Some people may favour yoga, a bath, hair and nails, building a treehouse; whatever your choices of resources, the golden rule is that it must be good for you and those around you – really good for you, not just an instant gratification good, but a true good. Only you know what that is for you.

There are some principles that resound in fulfilling that purpose. To be effective as a healing resource they must:

Enrich your life in some way and be considerate of others.

Be of pure intention; i.e. exercise is good but not if your intention is to look slimmer so you'll be accepted. That may be a consequence of your action but the resource itself needs to be driven by health, not ego.

Everyone needs some form of quieting the mind. Your choice of how you achieve that is limitless. Yoga, meditation, nature, a hot bath, enjoying the sun, or breathing deeply are some examples. The more often you do this one the richer the resource it provides.

Engage your mind, body, or spirit and your total resources must cover all bases. E.g. if you're a theoretical person you can't just choose resources that enrich the mind, your body and spirit can't be left out, otherwise the balance will be off and you will theorize into the illusion of healing rather than actual healing.

Focus on what you have already, rather than emphasising what you don't have.

Here are some examples of resources I use:

INTEGRATION

FIRSTLY, THE CONCEPT BEHIND THE EXPANSION IS TO RESOLVE conflict caused by beliefs. My belief that my life sucked and that my depression was the weight of the world, was preventing me from healing. To resolve that conflict within that was keeping me stuck, I changed how I thought about it. It was much more helpful to understand that being in depression gave me a reprieve to rest and subconsciously take a step back to review what was really going on. Well that is the superficial layer. Throughout this journey there was a much deeper challenge; the subconscious. Mini-conflicts came up every day that were caused by deep beliefs that I wasn't even aware of, and to heal I needed to find a way to access my subconscious to help resolve them. Once I accessed the deeper issue, I then needed to integrate it with my whole being. I still use to this day, many different techniques to achieve this.

EMDR

Eye Movement Desensitisation and Reprocessing. This technique is founded on evidence-based techniques that use eye movement to unlock trauma-related anxieties trapped within. PTSD is caused by an inability to process traumatic experience. You can sit and talk with a therapist all you like or try the initiatives in this book, however, if you don't access the trapped subconscious parts of the trauma, you will only heal so far. EMDRcanada.org is a helpful resource to learn more about this technique. I am no expert so won't go into detail. I just use the technique. I used the EMDR technique (or some form of it, as technically you need an EMDR therapist to administer it, but the principles are the same). When I was running and I wanted to release some rage, I could access the negative feeling and do a cross movement with my eyes (up / down, side to side) while I was feeling the emotion. I would breathe through whatever came up and I found that the running along with the eye movements helped release the physical manifestation of the emotion. It was very useful. This helped me come to the conclusion that I was in the wrong job at the adult training centre. The intense emotion was cleared so that I could think more clearly about what I wanted.

EFT TAPPING

Tapping is a combination of acupressure points and modern psychology. It balances your brain and your deeper emotions as well as your body energy. It is once again researched heavily and has much success in the treatment of PTSD. Resources: Tappingsolutionfoundation.org.

Tapping is using acupressure points while positively loving and accepting yourself for things that you feel are keeping you stuck. I have done a lot of shame release using this technique. It's almost like a confessional that spiritually wipes you clean, but can be used for any negative emotions or thoughts or flashbacks. Least resistance is key in that *what you resist persists (Carl Jung.)* If you completely accept whatever it is that you've done or not done, and whatever it is that is within you, including your traumatic experiences, then you can go with the flow of healing. You can't move on from what you don't acknowledge and this is a really good way to integrate those locked-away emotions from trauma. I even used this technique to feel better physically. I loved and accepted myself for my autoimmune disease, while loving and accepting myself for healing. I integrated them as whole. I am both healing and I have an autoimmune disease; the two were not as mutually exclusive as my subconscious made them out to be.

These are just some of the integrative tools I used that were very successful for me. I'm sure there are a myriad of other techniques. The ultimate goal is to integrate mind, body, and spirit as one. Trauma separates these for very good reason; you might be dead already if the intelligence of our protection mechanisms didn't step in when they needed to. However, to heal you must find a way to process that trauma on all levels of consciousness.

BRAINWAVES

There are some aspects of PTSD that are harder to reach, they cannot be counselled out, and you cannot follow any of these steps to heal. They are instead a deep misfiring of the brain created by the trauma. New-school theories are centering around the electrical activity of the brain. In the good old days, they used electric shock therapy (known as electroconvulsive therapy,) which had some success. Now, of course, with technological advances they can do much more than a sandblast to your brain. Many institutions are studying PTSD and its creation and affect on the brain. Most agree on the fact that the electrical impulses are different in people with PTSD. One school of thought offers beta blocker classes of drugs, while specifically recalling the traumatic events. The beta blocker helps to rewire the neural pathways while the patient is actively recounting the trauma. It desensitises and normalises the brain stimulation in a specific way. Other schools of thought use electrodes in specific areas of the brain to stop the excessive communication between brain communication centres. Some doctors are using narcotics in a controlled way under controlled sessions to once again specifically identify over-reactivity and desensitise that specific PTSD reaction.

There has been great success with these techniques. They are not provided by some backyard doctor; they have been studies on them at places like Massachusetts General Hospital. (Hardly a third-world backwater.)

They are often short healing methods, which do not require months or years-on-end of sessions. Most require just a few sessions to heal those deep trauma signals.

I will leave you to your own investigations of these, but my belief is that sometimes they are absolutely necessary to be able to truly heal. Once a neural pathway has formed –it is very difficult to un-form it unless it has some kind of intervention. My only suggestion is, try whatever works and is good for you. Be open to new, sometimes controversial techniques and keep safe.

ALLOWING GRATITUDE

It's a funny word, gratitude. I think of it as "attitude" with a "GRRR!" Gratitude can become a consequence of your mindfulness rather than putting in the extra effort to make a choice to be grateful. Being grateful doesn't have to be a hat you put on, it can more simply be an acknowledgement of what you feel after being mindful of painful feelings. (The painful feelings being the GRRR part, and the shift in attitude after that is the rest of the word.) You don't need to work so hard at it if you access the cause. Gratitude can be caused by the opening of your heart, which is caused by allowing emotions to flow through it; happy and painful. If you only focus on trying to be grateful without opening your heart it will fall flat, and as I have discovered, will make you feel like you always fall short despite your enthusiasm after watching Oprah. The gifts are already there for you to acknowledge, and if you feel they aren't there then perhaps your journey of being mindful hasn't been completed yet for this moment. It will always come.

When I start to feel even just a little bit better emotionally, simultaneously I feel this immense sense of gratitude for life and all that it brings; its joys, its pain, its suffering, and its compassion. It really resonates with me and who I want to be and who I believe I really am. It is an incredible, genuine essence of being grateful for life itself; my life, my experiences, every breath of every day of each of my forty- something years.

NATURE

Nature reminds us of perspective. Everything in nature is in perfect harmony, and when we notice it - it influences us harmoniously. I look at the stars often as they are a constant wherever I am in the world. I always surround myself in nature; the ocean, the mountains, trees, flowers, fauna. I didn't even mind my bear encounter, although I don't recommend seeking that one out. When I am feeling particularly crappy, nothing makes me feel better than strolling through the trails of the North Shore mountains in BC Canada. You see the city in the distance and get to see the daily struggles from an equal distance. Canadian astronaut Chris Hadfield said: *"I've had a chance to see something that is way outside everybody else's frame of reference and gives a perspective that is very different from everyone else's."*

Cleveland Dam North Vancouver

French River Ontario

PHYSICAL EXERCISE

Physical exercise is a must for all trauma survivors. If you curl up in a ball and stay there, so will your rage that is an inevitable by-product of trauma. I used to like running but can't do that anymore. Rock climbing will be my new exercise and I hope to buy a bike soon. I like swimming but over time it gets boring. I'd like something more fun.

Yoga balances both the physical and spiritual. It creates peace, inner balance, a meditative state, and puts you at one with the universe. I always thought these clichéd reflections were only for spacey, new age-y types: that is until my yoga class the other day. I am certainly not a yoga buff and in fact only started getting back to classes a week or two ago. In my second class I happened upon a truly spiritual moment. I must have hit all the components that accessed my deeper self, and I did feel at one with the universe. I felt my breath rise and fall through my whole body. I felt a peace where everything in the world was right, and I was doing exactly what I needed to be doing. I remembered my soul and felt all my fears and worries disintegrate. The following day I felt like I was floating on air; everything in the universe was supporting me, and my day at work went smoothly... but that was last week.

Last night I went to the same yoga class. I felt my sore back, the flies were annoying me, the crows in the trees were screeching, every pose was painful, and I could hardly hold them even though they were exactly the same as the previous week. I felt the cool wind and could not relax if I tried.

In every pose I drifted off into wondering what I was going to have for dinner later, or that I had to finish that report tomorrow at work, and why did this person say that to me. The next day at work I had incredible fatigue, every task I had was cumbersome, and all that could go awry did. Same class, same poses, totally different experience! It just goes to show you that just because you are at a yoga retreat, doesn't mean you are practicing spirituality. You can go through the exact same motions mindfully or you can get distracted by minor things, which at the end of the day don't really matter.

Life is like that. I find that HOW you do things is much more important than WHAT you do. I went to an indoor climbing class last week (a beginner's class) and as I was hanging on for dear life (when I didn't need to as I was adequately harnessed and supported), I felt stuck. I was supposed to stick to a particular colour handhold to challenge myself and show myself what level I was at, but I felt the next handhold of that colour was way too far for me to stretch to.

I was being encouraged by the instructor and I blocked her by saying, "I can't do it."

She said, "Well not with that attitude!"

And just out of spite, I maneuvered my way (quite easily I might add) over to the next appropriately coloured handhold.

She laughed and said, "I told you, you could do it."

I was shocked at what I could actually do. It looked too hard and hanging on with one hand as I looked at the next foothold up around my stomach I thought there was no way. But I was wrong. I wondered how many times in life I'd come up against a seemingly hard next step and I didn't do it because it looked too hard.

The next challenge was letting go when I was holding on so that my partner could learn how to "catch me" on belay. I had already felt how easy it was to catch someone if you did it correctly. Two fingers were all I'd needed. Yet when it came to physically letting go backwards off a wall, two storeys off the ground, once again, it was a challenge I had a lot of trouble approaching. And once again, once I did it, I realised just how easy it was.

Some things in life that seem uncomfortable or feel counter-intuitive and you feel like you could never achieve them, could be way easier than you think. And if you approach everything with such caution or distraction as I did this week, you may be missing out on some truly wonderful and peaceful moments. I felt fantastic after having climbed the wall and "letting go." Next week's class I will approach it differently, and I will also approach my life challenges in the same way. Checking in with how you approach anything in life is a good indicator of your regular pattern. Then seek out to break that pattern if it's not supportive of your healing. I want to get back to that peaceful yoga class. The only thing different was me! Having said that – any exercise is good, with or without the pure intention. Just being there, doing it, is helpful to unblock those traumatic cell memories.

MENTAL STIMULATION

Reading books, watching inspiring shows, going to seminars; all of these help. Find those that speak to you. Some of my favourite books are:

Deepak Chopra – *The Seven Spiritual Laws of Success*

Laurence Gonzales *Surviving Survival: The Art and Science of Resilience*

Gary Zukav – *The Heart of the Soul* (and the other *Soul* books, but this one is my fave)

John Edward – *What if God were the Sun?*

James Van Praagh – *Reaching to Heaven: A Spiritual Journey Through Life and Death* (Once again there are others but this one speaks to me the most.)

Tara Brach – *Radical Acceptance: Embracing Your Life with the Heart of a Buddha*

Neale Donald Walsch – *Conversations with God*

Viktor Frankl – *Man's Search for Meaning*

All of these books I have read many times, and I use them time and time again for reference. They are my go-to books. Others I have read and enjoyed and gotten a lot out of, but I wouldn't read them repeatedly like I do these ones. These were all life- changers for me. Keep reading, keep learning! The things that you are sensitive to are those things you need to work on or need to hear. While re-reading most of these books different things stand out to me at different times because of my own evolution. So keep the good ones handy, but have a list of feel-good books that you can go to, to lift you up at times of need. Books are an awesome sense of feeling that someone else has been through similar things.

FORGIVENESS
~ ANYWAY ~
People are often unreasonable, illogical, and self-centred;
Forgive them anyway.
If you are kind, people may accuse you of selfish, ulterior motives;
Be kind anyway.
If you are successful, you will win some false friends and some true enemies;
Succeed anyway.
If you are honest and frank, people may cheat you;
Be honest and frank anyway.
What you spend years building, someone could destroy overnight;
Build anyway.
If you find serenity and happiness, they may be jealous;
Be happy anyway.
The good you do today, people will often forget tomorrow;
Do good anyway.
Give the world the best you have, and it may never be enough;
Give the world the best you've got anyway.
You see, in the final analysis, it is between you and your God;
It was never between you and them anyway. ~
Attributed to Mother Theresa

Forgiveness! Now I understand the true meaning of forgiveness. This concept has been a constant battle for me of whether or not to forgive my perpetrators, but I have realised the reason why I could never come up with a suitable answer, is that I was asking the wrong question. Forgiveness, like many things, is an internal process, not an external one. I have mentioned in this book my reluctance to "forgive" my father, Peter, Simon, et al. I felt that I didn't want to make it about them. I didn't want to waste any more energy thinking anything about them; whether to forgive or not to forgive. I didn't want to squander another second on anything to do with any of my perpetrators.

Here's the issue with that: my life is still affected whether I deny this concept of forgiveness or not. By me NOT forgiving them, in some way I am *"drinking a poison and expecting them to be affected by it." - ANONYMOUS*. Harbouring any sort of negative emotion towards them is only going to affect me and those around me. Why on earth would they care if I was angry with them or not for what they did to me? That's laughable! That would assume that they had some compassion and understanding of what they did, which of course is an external factor. It totally diminishes my power over my feelings about the situation if I am expecting them to feel something from my anger or to have some remorse or guilt. I am giving away my power if I am expecting that my perpetrators are only linked to me by how I choose to feel about them. And if I am angry with them, then I am the only one drinking the poison. So how do I unlink this connection? I can't deny my feelings – that's just suppression as displayed in this book – and totally ineffective as a healing mechanism.

For some reason standing up for myself with regard to my relationship with Angie has unwittingly unblocked an ability to process my feelings about every relationship I've ever had. I no longer feel guilty about leaving David and the way that turned out; I no longer feel resentment and anger and rage towards Peter, Stephen, or even Simon, as I have been able to "forgive" all those connections. And I use the word forgiveness with every hesitation as it has so many pre-existing connotations, definitions, and meaning that I wouldn't want to connect with any of those people. So let me explain my own definition of what I mean by forgiveness.

It starts with a definition I've heard before but could never quite adapt to, mainly due to it missing some vital pieces. The starting point is that forgiveness means that I am no longer willing to hold onto any resentment about something that someone else did to me and that their behaviour is about them and has nothing to do with me. So all I have to address is me; not them. Their abuse of me is really just how they "projected" their dysfunctions on to me. It was never about me in the first place, so in a way – it's not even up to me to forgive them. That's their journey and as Mother Theresa says, that's between them and their God. My journey too is between me and God; it was never between me and them anyway.

Ok, now for the missing pieces. I could never resonate with that because it didn't matter how much I theorised about not resenting Peter, Simon, or my father, it would remain a cognitive function; a *theory* of forgiveness. Forgiveness does not exist in the mind, it is felt in the heart, so no amount of "thinking" differently about something was ever going to help. It would be like treating a symptom and never getting to the cause so the symptoms would always return. So unless I *did* something with my heart, then all the brains in the world could not integrate my being with the feeling of love and forgiveness. I could be Einstein and still not be able to achieve peace. Forgiveness doesn't take brains – it takes action. That is the right question. "What ACTION do I need to take to heal this heart?" The answer has been with me the whole time. I mentioned it earlier in the book, several times.

The action is to open my heart to feel the pain of my present moment entirely and allow whatever feelings are there to flow through me. No dodge ball, no dissociation, no disengagement from my present reality, just simply allowing myself to feel what is really in my heart, MY feelings, not what I think about someone else and what they did to me, but simply MY feelings about it. But wait! The definition for me does not stop there. Even with those two points – there's still more. I have tried every which way to connect with my feelings from the past; my anger, my rage, and allow them to flow – they never could. I may have accessed them but they never flowed through me. I thought it was a trust issue, I didn't have the right therapist, I didn't have friends who could stand by and catch me if I fell...but the reality is, I didn't need any of that. I didn't need to go back in time to the traumatic events and pull out my rage.

So I realised the third part of my definition: Only through a present feeling of hardship, or emotional confrontation can you truly let go of a past one. The past is gone. It doesn't matter how accurately you are remembering it – that in itself happens in the brain. Like I said, forgiveness does not happen in the brain, so how can you access it there? My PTSD can access the feelings *like* they are in the present, but the truth is they are not here now. I am not being gang raped now, or beaten or shot at or betrayed or abandoned now. They do affect my present moment but the event I am upset about cannot be brought back irrespective of how real my triggered feelings are. I could cry up a storm over the gang rape, remembering every detail, every step, every smell, and every painful moment. But in reality it is not happening to me right now, so I can't recreate the feeling exactly enough to be able to release it.

With Angie leaving I felt all of those feelings. I felt abandonment, pain, betrayal, anger, hurt, sadness, all these things in that moment for leaving Angie. These were the real feelings in the moment. They weren't from the past but they were the same feelings. Anger is anger, sadness is sadness, it doesn't matter what the cause is – the feeling itself is no different. Then I could allow my heart to open and allow the feelings to flow through for the first time, and I let the flood gates burst open. I did not deny it as I had done many times before. In that activity of breaking up with Angie and letting my heart feel every millisecond of pain, I was able to access my heart at such a deep level that I could allow it to resonate through ALL of my fears, ALL of my pain - great and small. Once you have opened your heart in that way you can't block it again. That's like closing the dam after the water has broken through. You can't bring the water back. So forgiveness for me is not about talking to Peter or Dad or anyone, it's simply a process of allowing my dam/n wall, (pun intended) i.e. my heart to open and release every emotion that's in it until the water flow balances out and stops itself. I couldn't stop the flow now even if I wanted to.

So with all the present-moment feelings it has to be something big enough where your heart is forced to reconcile itself. As I said before, you can choose in that moment to let the flood waters through or to keep your fingers in the dyke and hope that it holds a little longer – but it will break. This is not a pleasant experience. It hurts like hell, but better to express a little pain now than hold onto a lifetime of anger that could continue until *you* break. Maybe a nervous breakdown, maybe cancer, maybe broken relationships – whatever the form, the dam must break. It's simple physics. Something builds up until it has enough force that it either spills over the top like the Japan tsunami, or it breaks the walls entirely like in Hurricane Katrina. It's simple physics. You can only build up strong negative emotions for so long. I was forty-something years old. I could not hold it any longer. Something was gonna break. And now I feel the greatest peace I've ever experienced in my life. Yes, it still hurts, but it will not kill me. And I KNOW it will get better.

A New Beginning

I STARTED THIS BOOK IN 2012. TODAY IS APRIL 1ST 2017, FIVE years later and I pretty much finished the book on the same day I started. I'm sure you can feel the difference in my writing from those first days to now. I have my E.M.P.O.W.E.R. acronym and its relevant associated words tattooed on my arm, so I can recall it at any time by looking at it. It's my emotional emergency heal kit in an easy to follow acronym. I have a website and a blog. My dog is still the love of my life, which is probably why I don't have a girlfriend yet as there's no room in the bed, but perhaps one day soon she will come. My awesome job still remains. It still enriches me every day and I am excited to go to work. I am equally excited to come home and work on my writing. I am still seeking the appropriate treatment for my autoimmune and fibromyalgia, which is very exciting as I now realize that I had been in much more pain than I'd thought. Sometimes things only exist in the presence of their opposites – if I haven't been out of pain in years, how can I know what my regular pain feels like and what no pain feels like? Could I start running that marathon after all? Who knows where this will lead? All I can be sure of is that it will be healthier, despite the fact that I can hardly walk at the moment.

When I review my life to date, I realize that I used to feel like I'd been robbed of a fulfilling life. After all, PTSD insidiously permeates every cell of your being – every decision is coloured by it, and I have to say it's not a great life manager. I know I could have been a paramedic, or a police officer, or even a doctor, were it not for the PTSD and abuse affecting my life. PTSD does not make healthy choices, but when I get down to what's really important in life, all I wanted from the start was to be a contributing member of society, offering my skills as I have them, and connecting with others. When I look at those ambitions next to the life I've led – I realize that I did have all these things. In fact, with my experiences, I can contribute and connect at a greater depth than I ever could have, had I led a "normal" life. I am contributing my brutal story – I am sharing it with others. I didn't have to save the world to contribute, I saved myself and shared it with the world. That's enough! And in fact, it's more than I ever could have given as a paramedic. I am connecting with others at a deep level. I have reason to appreciate the great things I have in life; like my excellent job, my dog, my friends, and my family. I have learned so much in this lifetime about myself and about humanity, and I have succeeded as a human.

And look, here I am at the end of the book and the beginning of my next journey. I feel almost as though my life is just starting. I feel like I could have felt as a teenager going out into the world seeking my place in it, but what I have offers so much more. My life has filled the pages of this book with experience and hope and creativity that I can now share. I am happy. I live my healing initiatives, empowered by my experiences.

FIFTY AND BEYOND

I DIDN'T HAVE A VOICE FOR SO LONG. SCARRED BY SEVERE trauma, rape, violence, emotional abuse, and abandonment, I struggled with life. It was a battle of wills. Will I survive? Will I fit in? Will anyone hear me anyway? I tried every possible kind of help; medical, counselling practitioners, hospital, friends, groups, books, and healing treatments – I tried them all. It wasn't until my forty-third year that I realised the only fight going on was within myself. I was not at war with the world, just with me. Traumas had long since passed, however, the residue lingered. Having said that, trauma gave me as much as it took away, but I wasn't noticing the gifts, only the void.

I found a way to step out of the darkness and live freely for the first time. It took all of my forty-three and a half years to do so, and then it took a little while to put it all into practice. I am now forty-eight. I am strong, I am empowered, and I am living an awesome life, but it doesn't need to take that long. I am sharing my story; my trials and tribulations so that others don't need to take so long to find their voice, their place in the world, and their validity. I share my story so that others who feel alone know that their isolation is an illusion; there are others in similar circumstances, there is hope, and there is a way. I reiterate that I am not a trained counsellor or psychologist; my strategies are just what has worked for me over the years. My approach may not work for everyone, but if it worked for me it means, by the spirit of humanity that it will translate for others.

You may not have suffered the same things in the same way, but I found a path that many can share, and hopefully the journey won't take forty-eight years. I am more excited by every decade that passes. I feel more and more connected with life and the people in it. I see my struggles as opportunities to learn and heal. TIEWIN! I have come full circle within the five years that I have been documenting my journey. Healing is really not about overcoming all your challenges to lead a happy life; it is really to be happy with the life you are leading with all its complications. This is an important distinction. I used to strive to be better, stronger, happier. I would read self help books and really click with what they were saying but then I would find disappointment when I couldn't end up like the author where life was blissful. I didn't realise that contentedness can look like pain, it can feel like courage and it can come in the worst moments of your life.

My soul mate Sebastien and I at our favourite spot in Capilano Regional Park. This was taken in 2011. I was there again just this morning in 2017.

Printed in Canada